Align is more than a church st [illegible] for the pilgrim who has been called to set a new trail ablaze in a different direction from the one previously walked. This journey of leadership shared in *Align* is a journey of a weathered traveler of sleepless nights, countless whiteboard sessions, with his face to the ground in humility before God, multiple hard conversations, but one radiating truth . . . God was in it all, and his church responded!

Ed Newton, lead pastor at Community Bible Church, San Antonio, Texas, and author of *Breathe Again: Inhaling God's Goodness, Exhaling His Blessings*

Align combines real-world examples with biblical clarity to take discipleship from the early church to today's church. This journey will not only encourage your heart but also inform your steps. The Lord has called us all to be disciples and disciple makers. Therefore, by aligning your focus and ministry through the pages of this book, you will become keenly aware of the importance that Jesus placed on following him and his ways.

Gregg Matte, senior pastor at Houston's First Baptist Church, Houston, Texas, and author of *Difference Makers, Unstoppable Gospel,* and *I Am Changes Who I Am*

Navigating change in any organization can be hard. It is especially difficult in churches. To do it right and in a way that honors Jesus and the people one shepherds, it takes time, intentionality, care, and a stubborn willingness to be obedient to the mission God has called you to—whatever the cost may be. This is the journey that Matt Roberson has walked. *Align* is honest, raw, and most of all, filled with hope. If you are thinking about transitioning your church or leading change in your organization, this book is for you.

Jarrett Stephens, senior pastor at Champion Forest Baptist Church, Houston, Texas, and author of *The Always God: He Hasn't Changed and You Are Not Forgotten*

There is an epidemic of American churches finding themselves at the crossroads of last breath and new life, disillusioned and fractured. *Align* is a firsthand account of fighting for unity. This book is an encouragement for a local church in a vulnerable spot or a leader trying to forge a new and healthy direction.

Marshall Hall, worship pastor at Northland Church, Longwood, Florida

The call to make disciples is a marathon, not a sprint. In a culture addicted to speed and streamlining, *Align* highlights the biblical call to intentional relationships through the local church. In fact, I appreciate the challenge to come back to the biblical roots of relational discipleship. *Align* pushes us to consider a gospel adventure through the marathon of deepening relationships in the local church—a call back to relational gospel advancement. I am challenged to bring this kind of authenticity to our Mission in Owasso and Tulsa.

Chris Wall, senior pastor, First Baptist Owasso/The Mission Church, Tulsa, Oklahoma

True discipleship exists within the framework of personal and intimate relationships with one another. Matt Roberson reveals how advancing beyond church tradition is vital to achieving authentic and healthy relationships within the church body.

Wes Hampton, Gaither Vocal Band, Nashville, Tennessee

Align: A Church's Shift from Tradition to Mission is simple, readable, and applicable. This book is a must read! Matt's experience and journey is compelling and life giving. *Align* will be required reading for our staff and leadership.

Keith Strasburger, lead pastor, Parkview Baptist Chuch, Lexington, Nebraska

MATT ROBERSON

ALIGN

A Church's Shift from

Tradition to Mission

ISBN: 979-8-9865314-0-3 (Paperback)
ISBN: 979-8-9865314-1-0 (Kindle)
ISBN: 979-8-9865314-2-7 (ePub)

Editor: Jody Janz

No transitions happen without the blood, sweat, and tears of many. I dedicate this book to the men and women of The MET Church in Houston, Texas. I am so grateful for the staff who lived this story out and contributed to this project not only with written words but also with hours of relational investment and change management. I applaud the people who had to overcome personal obstacles to ensure the success of what Jesus called us to do as well as those who no longer call The MET their home because of changes that took place along the way.

This book is another testimony to the grace that God freely allows us to engage. It is a story peppered with victories as well as pain points. But the fruit that is being born has been worth every second, every hard conversation, every difficult question, and every painful decision. None of it would be possible without an amazing team of dedicated staffers and church volunteers. They are the reason this church continues to shine in her city. They are the reason she continues to bear fruit. They are the catalysts, and they all deserve to celebrate the win that is The MET Church!

CONTENTS

Introduction

THE TENSION

My heritage of growing up in church has always been valuable to me. My dad pastored small churches in Texas and Mississippi, and then in Illinois and Idaho for most of my formative years. The musty halls of those churches were my playground, my hiding places, and even my formal schooling. I was raised on gospel music, singing harmony with my sisters and mom and dad on the stage at church for as long as I can remember. I memorized the Scriptures in Bible drill, ate hundreds of meals at church-wide potlucks, and was disciplined by countless older ladies in my church, one being Miss Miriam, who was our adopted grandmother. I appreciate the standard of doctrine and strong faith that my parents imparted to me. I have memories of church being a place I enjoyed, a safe place. I learned to respect and revere it from a young age.

Though I have so much to appreciate about my church heritage and my denominational framework, I also now see some ways that it was lacking. Some of those gaps became even more obvious due to the cultural shifts over the past several years as America moved away from morality and Judeo-Christian beliefs toward universalism and a post-Christian society. The gap between culture and the traditional American church is now significant. Culture has deconstructed religious life all together. And it's exposing a real problem.

Something foundational is broken in your church and in my church. As Jim Putman, senior pastor of Real Life Ministries in Post Falls, Idaho, once said at a conference, "The church isn't a winning team!" Sunday school, Bible study, and small groups are producing educated and even dedicated followers of Jesus, but not necessarily mature disciples of Jesus. Jim followed up his statement with another: "We divorced the message of Jesus from the methods of Jesus but still expected the results of Jesus." Our seminaries prepare young ministers with the skills to exegete Scripture but not necessarily the relational tools to weave those truths into the fabric of everyday life.

As a result, we act like Jesus' command to love God and love others is a race, with the latter in a distant second. But we cannot keep pretending that our relationships with others don't matter so long as we are "good with God." It's a contradiction. Authentic, transformative, Great Commission-style discipleship occurs best through the meaningful relationships we develop with one another. Understanding this concept radically shifts how we "do church." It affects how we organize the church, how we lead the church, why we go to church, and what the church offers to our lost world.

It's not our worship services that change the world. Ancient hymns or modern worship don't change it. Our pastors' sermons don't give people the tools to transform their lives. Those may be factors in whether a guest returns or stays; however, true transformation and true winning in the kingdom realm will never come through a gathering on a weekend. When we marginalize church to weekly classes and services, weeks turn into months and months into years, until we make a startling realization: we, and the people who sit next to us, look exactly the same week after week, and never feel equipped to follow Christ's command to make disciples. And as leaders, we can't put our finger on why.

Our system of how we do church is broken. People walk in and out. The number of converts ebbs and flows with the seasons, but no matter what clever new sermon series we come up with or exciting curriculum we implement into our children's ministry classes, very little actually changes. For the most part people are still ill-equipped, keeping silent when it comes to sharing their stories about how the gospel changed their lives. What's worse, we appear comfortable—and in some cases, justified—in doing so because of a noisy, busy culture.

But this is not the model Jesus emulated for us during his time on earth. Jesus was all about people. And we should be too. His love for people wasn't something he manufactured; it was something he embodied. Loving people wasn't simply something he did; it was who he was.

Our churches don't necessarily look this way. Could it be that we have been lulled to sleep by the pattern and monotony of traditional church? Somewhere along the way we traded people for programs and mission for metrics. As we pushed toward the next trending leadership model, we still lost ground. Where is transformational life change as the norm in our churches? Where is engagement of fruitful, missional living as disciples of Christ? Where is the vibrancy and love-fueled action in our churches that we see in Acts 2?

That's the reason for this book. Our quiet times and church attendance have not produced the culture that we see in the churches of the New Testament. Thus, I propose a change. New Testament discipleship—mine and yours—only finds true fruit in the context of relationship with others. It's not just transferring knowledge or logging time in a church building. It is the sharing of life. What would it look like if we aligned our lives as well as the organizations we lead to the message and methods of Jesus?

Maybe you resonate with the frustration and stagnation of church. The MET is a church that's more than fifty years old with a rich heritage. Some of our current members have been there for the entirety of that journey. They have lived through some highs and some lows, as every church has. They speak of seasons of fruitfulness in an evangelism focus, well-attended Christmas productions, and a reputation of giving generously to overseas missions. We navigated the "worship battle" days of traditional versus contemporary and hopped on the "multisite" train in the early 2000s. But we looked like almost every other Baptist church out there. Church felt stale and common and familiar. We were in pursuit of a new thing. We needed a shift, but to what?

Around that time, our senior pastor and a team attended a DiscipleShift 1 (at that time called Immersion 1) conference in Post Falls, Idaho. While we were there, God birthed a new path in us as leaders. The conference proved to be the catalyst to help us move ahead, attempting to lead this church into her new season of life and ministry. With a rich Southern Baptist background and anchors in certain programmatic thinking, it would not be an easy climb. God called us to shift to a better model.

The entire two-day intensive pointed us back to Jesus' methods for making disciples—through relationships. It might sound basic and simple, but it was transformational. We had lost sight of the call of Jesus to his bride, the church. Over those forty-eight hours, we uncovered what a disciple of Jesus was and was not. We defined what it meant to be a disciple of Jesus. We examined the life of Jesus, the time he spent with his disciples, and the intentionality with which he led. So much of our church's identity was tied up in what used to be. The new trajectory would be challenging for us, but we made the commitment. Over time we moved from being a "Sunday's coming" culture to a "discipleship first" culture—at all costs. That conviction had to resonate in the hearts of all of us at the senior leadership table, which was no small task. It never is.

Paul modeled this when he said to the church, "We loved you so much that we shared with you not only God's Good News but our own lives, too" (1 Thess. 2:8, NLT). It is time we make our priority the people who occupy our seats. The shift to which I testify in this book is a giving away of us as leaders for the purpose of making disciples who make disciples. This sounds simple, but it is not as easy as it appears. Becoming vulnerable with people within our congregations requires great risk.

In my opinion, the current model of traditional American church is easier on the leader. Within this model I declare how everyone should live all while having zero people to keep me accountable on whether I am living that way too. But the better model that we see in Scripture requires me to sit in a circle of other believers, confess my limitations, and allow others to minister to me in my own discipleship journey.

I knew that submitting to this new discipleship process was critical. I would be unable to lead people where I wasn't willing to go myself. I had to make personal changes in my theology, changes in my philosophy of ministry, and then align our organization accordingly. This book is the story of alignment—an alignment of my heart, an alignment of the heart of our organization, and an alignment that moved us from tradition to mission.

Part 1

RELATIONAL ALIGNMENT

1

ALIGN MY HEART

I had been working on staff at The MET for about four years before our former pastor left. I remember the transition being full of turmoil, as the pastor had been there for nearly twenty years, and the change was sudden. My attention quickly focused on the congregation and providing a sense of stability and consistency for them that had been lacking. My wife and I had felt the warning in Ezekiel 34:2: "Woe to the shepherd who only takes care of themselves! Should not shepherds take care of the flock?" We felt we had received a clear invitation to stay and care for this vulnerable flock. My thought was to remain a calming, familiar voice in the interim, knowing the calling of a new leader would give clarity as to what my next step would be.

As often happens when God reveals a change, only one clear step is revealed at a time. About six months into that interim period, I read 1 Peter 5:2–4: "Care for the flock that God has entrusted to you. Watch over it willingly, not grudgingly—not for what you will get out of it, but because you are eager to serve God. Don't lord it over the people assigned to your care but lead them by your own good example. And when the Great Shepherd appears, you will receive a crown of never-ending glory and honor" (NLT). Through this scripture and others, I felt the Spirit heavily impress upon me to submit my résumé to the search team. You need to understand how ludicrous and irrational this was. I had not completed my seminary degree, nor had I ever pastored a church. God's entrusting this congregation to me was breathtaking, scary, and humbling. And I knew that not everyone I was doing life with at the time would agree or even understand what God was calling me to do.

God affirmed this call again and again to me and my wife. The whisper of the Spirit spoke from the Psalms: "LORD, you alone are my portion and my cup; you make my lot secure. The boundary lines have fallen for me in pleasant places; surely, I have a delightful inheritance. I will praise the LORD , who counsels me; even at night my heart instructs me. I keep my eyes always on the LORD . With him at my right hand, I will not be shaken" (16:5–8).

Finally, I'll never forget reading the story of Jesus and Peter on the beach in John 21, when Jesus asked three different times if Peter loved him. Peter answered with an emphatic "Yes!" each time, and each time Jesus told Peter, "Feed my sheep." Then Jesus gave him one last command, "Follow me," and Peter saw his fellow disciple, John, and asked, "What about him?" This exchange struck me. Most of my concerns with walking in this new reality were about how this decision would affect those with whom I was doing ministry. I had assumed too much concern for those around me rather than prioritizing the next step I knew God was calling me to take.

God again communicated to me clearly that I was being set apart for this. It's as if God answered my concerns in the same way Jesus answered Peter: "If I want him to remain alive until I return, what is that to you? You must follow me!" (John 21:22). There it was again, God's clear command to me: "What I do with your friend is not up to you. It's up to me. Are you going to follow me?"

All these things resonated deeply within me. As God stirred my soul, I went to the elders and shared how I sensed the Holy Spirit leading me to make my name available as the next pastor. They looked at each other strangely. They had all these other candidates who had submitted résumés from all over the country, most of whom had more education than I did. However, they asked me to submit my résumé, even though I'd already been on staff for over four years, and to work with hiring agents as they continued to conduct interviews. The process dragged on for what seemed like forever, yet God continued to affirm his calling not just to me but to our eldership and search team as well.

Approximately fifteen months later, the eldership requested that Jennifer and I have a formal interview with them. On the day of the interview, Jennifer read in 1 Kings 2:3, where David commissioned Solomon to be entrusted with the leadership of Israel. He challenged Solomon to be strong and walk in obedience to God's decrees and commands: "Do this so that you may prosper in all you do and wherever you go." Solomon responded in humility, thanking God for his mercy and kindness to him.

He begged God for a discerning heart to govern the people and to discern what to do. Solomon's feelings of inadequacy in his calling resonated with Jennifer and me. But his father's blessing confirmed Solomon's next step.

That night, we met at the home of one of our elders. We ate a wonderful meal together prepared by the elder's wife and sat in their living room. The group then freely asked all their questions to us—about marriage, kids, and personal spiritual testimonies. Jennifer shared how she had seen God cultivate a pastor's heart in me over the years, and that the time between the former pastor's departure and the new pastor's selection had given her space to confirm that call as well. As the night ended, we closed in prayer, asking God to illuminate continually the path for all of us, and then we left.

A few days later, the elders asked that Jennifer and I meet them in my office the next morning at 7:30 a.m. After we arrived, they said, "We have collectively sought the Lord and have asked that he make his will abundantly clear to us. We feel confident that he has done that and shown us that you are our next senior pastor. We all want to show you what God did." They each read a passage of Scripture that God had used to confirm the call. As the final elder began to read Jeremiah 1:4–10, I bowed my head with emotion.

> The word of the LORD came to me, saying, "Before I formed you in the womb I knew you, before you were born, I set you apart; I appointed you as a prophet to the nations."

"Alas, Sovereign LORD," I said, "I do not know how to speak; I am too young."

But the LORD said to me, "Do not say, 'I am too young.' You must go to everyone I send you to and say whatever I command you. Do not be afraid of them, for I am with you and will rescue you," declares the LORD.

Then the LORD reached out his hand and touched my mouth and said to me, "I have put my words in your mouth. See, today I appoint you over nations and kingdoms to uproot and tear down, to destroy and overthrow, to build and to plant."

I was undone. Those were all concerns I had expressed in previous interviews and conversations, and God answered them with a specific passage that had been meaningful to me for some time. Jennifer looked at me while I tried to recover from the weight of the situation, and she said, "Do you know what passage that is? That's the passage your dad preached from at your ordination service." She then asked, "Do you know what today is?" and I quickly realized it was the anniversary of my father's death. Again, a father's blessing had confirmed the next step of obedience for a son.

The words of blessing from David to his son, the bold commissioning of Jeremiah that had been read over me by my father, and the timing and confirmation through the elders and God's Word were undeniable. It was one of the most powerful and providential moments of my life. To this day I can't tell you why God chose me, but despite my lack of formal education or experience as a senior pastor, God planted in me what he wanted me to do with The MET. He had called me to lead the church to a place we had never been, and we wouldn't get there unless I was willing to go first.

That's what leaders do. I'm not the most gifted communicator, orator, or writer, but I am driven to help people understand and embrace what it means to live life with God and each other in meaningful relationships. That value has made the difference in the success of The MET Church.

Leaders Go First

Shortly thereafter, I approached an intern at our church about meeting regularly. *Why would the senior pastor want to meet with me?* He couldn't process why I wanted to meet with him personally. On the day of our first meeting, I walked in with only a Bible and the book we were reading tucked under my arm. When I sat down, the intern looked around expecting to see me carry a phone or a computer, ready to become distracted at any moment. Instead, I had made a promise to myself: I would be fully present with him during our time together. As we talked, we discussed the book but segued quickly into life. I got to know more about his preferences, his backstory, his upbringing, his immediate family situation, and so much more. Most importantly, I saw him—*really* saw him.

As the intern got up to leave, he said, "Thanks, Pastor Matt, I know you're incredibly busy. I really appreciated meeting with you today. This isn't normal."

I sat for a moment in silence and wondered why a young man who had so much leadership potential would be awestruck as to why I wanted to spend time with him. I believe it's because of what we often see in leadership roles. Many leaders have multiple layers between themselves and the people, whether it's the staff or the members. These leaders don't often get to know those within the organization. Sure, it could be that leaders can be prideful, but often it's fear. Fear that if we, as leaders, embrace getting to know the people, or worse yet, them getting to know us, they won't like what they see. Fear that if something were to change, go wrong, or if we hit a relational bump in the road, the pain will not be worth the knowing. That's how most of us have been brought up believing about leadership.

The model for so many is that leadership is done from a platform, a talking head, or a boardroom. It's more about how much money we make, or who we know who can get us those good seats at the games. It has become more about information and less about influence. The idea of knowing others and being known by others has often been set aside. A significant fallacy exists with this way of thinking. If we're honest with ourselves, success in leadership requires serious relational acumen. A leader must learn when the agenda leads and when the relationship leads. A leader must be able to distinguish the temperature of a meeting, a lunch conversation, or a coffee. And it can be grueling to give someone your full self: your presence, your undivided attention, your life.

Jesus exemplified leadership through relationship. Whether it was with the disciples, his friends, or with his Father, Jesus always gave the gift of his full self. Even though Jesus, the Son of God, was divine, he willingly set his title aside to humble himself for the sake of real, meaningful relationship with you and me. His was a better model. The better model is leadership through intimacy and connection, not simply vision and pace.

And if I expect the people whom I lead to live this way, the hard reality is that it begins with me. The intimacy I desire for God's people is the same intimacy I must model as a leader. This concept is foreign to so many leaders. It seems like it would slow us down or prevent us from doing all and being all we can be. Yet, it's the path Jesus showed toward missional living—laying one's life down for the good of others. Being a good leader means walking out life together and trusting the process. It's about meaningful relationships. Not pseudo-relationships, acquaintances, or transactional relationships, but authentic, meaningful relationships.

Elder Culture

In the early months of my new pastor transition, elders' meetings looked like a typical board meeting with a prayer at the beginning. I came equipped with my agenda, ready to work through the important items of business that were urgent for the month. We started with the typical niceties and handshakes, then they took their seats around the conference table. As we began the meeting, I opened with a word of prayer, then conducted our normal church business. Everyone was cordial, sharing their opinions on various church business items. A few hours later, the meeting was over, and one by one the elders filed out in the same way they came in.

One evening as I cleaned up afterward, I felt that something wasn't right in our meetings. Everything went fine, and the agenda accomplished what we set out to do. By all accounts, this was a win in my eyes. But as I reflected further, I realized our elder table didn't reflect the mission that we were working so hard to integrate to every corner of the church. I had served alongside these men for many years, but I knew very little about their lives. I could name their wives and their children's names, but I didn't *know* them, at least not in the way a pastor should know the flock entrusted to his care. I couldn't name their most recent struggle, or even their current prayer requests. In fact, I couldn't tell you much about them at all.

After praying and repenting before the Lord, I promised him that I would take a vested interest in my leaders. When the elders arrived for the next meeting, I intentionally asked each one a question to get to know the men better: "How is Elizabeth's basketball season going?" "Did your grandson get that scholarship he was applying for?" "How did that doctor's report turn out?" We rejoiced together on a few answers to prayer, and a few prayer concerns surfaced for the men personally. I made mental notes of what we discussed.

We began the meeting with a word of prayer. Following the prayer, I asked: "What has God done in your life in the past week?" Soon each elder shared about all the ways God was using them in their workplaces, their communities, and their families. The atmosphere changed that night, and as we checked off the last business item, we were amazed to learn the meeting had been four hours long!

I tell you this story not to brag about how our church has it all together, or that we have cracked the magic code on how to do church well. If you have led in a senior capacity in any organization, you are fully aware that those meetings can be cumbersome and tiring, always centering on topics such as profitability, attendance numbers, facility planning, investment portfolios, etc. But our board meetings had to move from solely being driven by an agenda to being more centered on Jesus' method for making disciples in meaningful relationships, especially at the top. That meant the entire structure of the meeting had to look different. Not only did we need to integrate and model the very thing that had become our central mission, but we also needed to fortify and strengthen the spiritual protection of our church.

We now refer to the elder board as the spiritual covering of our church. The goal was to move it from being a transactional, agenda-driven meeting to one that cultivated our spiritual development and accountability as well as our love for each other and the Lord. In other words, we had to build relationship with each other around the table—real relationship. In that spirit and environment, we then turned our attention to managing people, putting out fires, and solving problems.

Let me give you an overview of what our meeting looked and felt like in the new reality. We started at 5:30 p.m. sharing a meal together. An elder's wife cooked for us and brought the meal to our meeting area. As we sat and ate, the small talk quickly moved to family talk. We spoke of jobs, the successes and challenges of our children, our relationships with our spouses, and how we needed prayer and accountability in so many unique areas of life. I shared some Scripture as we ate dessert, and we dialogued about how the Holy Spirit was speaking to us in that moment—great conversation centered on meaningful relationship with God and each other. We took a quick break, and then came back to discuss some pressing issues within the church body we needed to work through. Before we knew it, 9:00 p.m. rolled around and we were tired, but rather than being worn down, we felt full—physically and spiritually. We also felt compassion toward one another and knew how to pray for each other and who needed a check-in that week. I remember one elder pulling me aside later, with a tear in his eye as he told me, "Our meetings have never been like this."

There it was—the beginning of something new. This was one of the most valuable and critical things that shifted at The MET. It is undeniably valuable to have this spiritual covering by men who do not lead primarily with their business acumen and monetary success but rather seek primarily to grow as disciples of Jesus Christ. They submit to him and each other as they seek God's direction in leading the church. This has been a foundational stone in our church's new identity.

2

ALIGN THE LANGUAGE

Language matters. No matter what capacity in which you lead, you must align your language to the mission and vision you are setting. As we embarked on this path of relational discipleship, both of those words required new meanings. For example, "relational," at least in the southern parts of the United States, can simply mean hospitable. We see it in our context all the time. The South is notorious for platitudes and niceties on the surface, ensuring people feel good when they are in your presence. However, it is also common for that same "relational" style to prevent people from truly knowing each other.

"Discipleship" is another word that means so many different things in different cultures that it can often be confusing. For Baptist churches in the South, discipleship can mean a Wednesday or Sunday night program where people do an in-depth Bible study under a pastor's teaching. It could also mean traditional Sunday school. For the most part, it tends to be synonymous with teaching and learning, and that's good. However, there is so much more to it than that.

True relational discipleship is about being known by God and being known by others. It is not just my understanding of Scripture but also the accountability that comes with living next to someone who loves me and wants what God wants for my life. And that's just the tip of the iceberg. Being honest about ourselves often flies in the face of the southern cultural conditioning we experience in this part of the world. We had a lot of aligning to do in this key area, otherwise "I'm fine" would be as deep as our mission would permeate.

The Why Behind the What

When Jesus died, the veil that divided the holy of holies from the rest of the temple where men dwelt was torn in two. We often gloss over this statement, but it carries much weight for us as leaders, particularly as pastors and disciples. When the veil was torn, it signified no more division between God and humanity. Before, only the high priest, the mediator between God and the people, could go behind the veil. But upon Jesus' death, the essence of the relationship between God and humanity changed. Everyone now had a right to enter the throne room of grace with confidence!

The same is true with leaders in a church today. God has granted a new kind of access today just as he did when the veil tore in two. This is critical for leaders to understand; we must grant God and others access into our lives. It's messy, risky, and makes us vulnerable, but transformation follows. The fruit that is produced is rich, sweet, and well worth the risk.

Consider some of the relationships throughout Scripture. God created Adam and Eve to work together in the garden. They were equal in value but had different roles. When working together they achieved God's purpose for them of filling the earth and subduing it. As a leader, I may have more accountability before God because of my calling as a shepherd and teacher, but at my core I am not more valuable because of my role. All Christians are equal in stature and value to God, but they have different roles to play in his kingdom. And more than that, those roles are only fully realized in relationship to God and each other.

This means we cannot lead well and stay relationally immature. It takes all the parts of the body working together, valuing each other deeply, and living life with each other in community and loving connection to truly realize our potential. God wants leaders who understand this truth to rise up in his church. So many things pull our attention away from meaningful relationships, and we have lost the sacred context for discipleship and maturity amid our distraction.

Look at the life of Jesus. He loved his disciples and became so close to them by the end of his ministry that he referred to them as brothers. Imagine Jesus' willingness to humble himself enough to call his betrayers, Judas and Peter, his brothers. That humility was one of Jesus' crowning attributes during his time here on earth. It underscored his relational life with his mother, his disciples, his other followers, and his Father. He showed a level of humility that had never been seen before, and that gave birth to true, meaningful relationship—intimacy with those whom he loved and led.

When is the last time you did a relational inventory? Sit down and write the names of those people you interact with in life most. How would you characterize those relationships? What about those you lead? Are they transactional? Are they encouraging? Are they simply time fillers? Or are they truly meaningful? Do you really have that level of connection and intimacy with the people you lead? What about those who live under your roof? Do they really know you? Living life this way is risky. It takes trust and courage to experience intimacy in a way only a select few experience. But if we're going to model our leadership after Jesus himself, we must take the risk.

Have you seen Disney's *The Mandalorian*? There's a saying that each Mandalorian says to one another: "This is the way."[1] This is the mantra of those committed to relational discipleship: when it comes to relationships, this is the way. In my initial years of becoming senior pastor, this was one of the most important lessons we learned: fighting for a relationship above everything else is the way of Jesus. Remember Jesus' words in John 13:35: "A new command I give you: Love one another. As I have loved you, so you must love one another. By this everyone will know that you are my disciples, if you love one another." This is what mattered most to Jesus. The more than fifty "one anothers" in Scripture all reveal the importance that God places on relationship. Everything Jesus preached was reinforced by the life he lived. Jesus himself restored fellowship with humanity through his death on the cross, the ultimate fight for relationship. Relationship wasn't just a means to an end; it was the end itself.

Obstacles to Relationship

For the most part we are extremely risk averse, especially when it comes to having hard conversations, wading through hurt feelings, and managing our personal image. Obstacles often disorient us, speak lies into our thought processes, and taint the waters of building relational equity with one another. We have adopted "Sprite theology," which teaches that "Image is everything." In fact, the messages of commercials, media channels, and the like push us in the opposite direction of meaningful relationships, and our culture feels it. The church feels it too.

As leaders we must ask ourselves if we are loving people or using people. Are people simply considered assets in a strategic conversation, or are they the strategy itself? The religious leaders of the day once asked Jesus to define the greatest commandment in the Law:

> Jesus replied: "'Love the Lord your God with all your
> heart and with all your soul and with all your mind.' This
> is the first and greatest commandment. And the second
> is like it: 'Love your neighbor as yourself.' All the Law
> and the Prophets hang on these two commandments."
> (Matt. 22:36–40)

The dilemma of loving others for so many of us is exposed in Jesus' brilliant response. How are we supposed to love others when we don't even know if we love ourselves? We must do the hard work, the searching of the soul, the time in solitude with the Lord to truly work out our identity in Christ.

One major obstacle we face is our church culture's value system. The American church is more corporate in nature than ever before. This is a real fight for those of us who lead in the American church. Of course, the drive for numeric growth is not evil by any means, and each number represents a soul. But if numeric growth is the priority, it can compete with the call to lead people to full maturity in Christ. This development happens in relationship. Rather than putting on the CEO hat and strategizing how to create better programs, we must slow down and invest first in those we lead. We must love. We must love ourselves, and that must inform our loving of others.

Other obstacles could be our own past, the lack of health in our homes or organizations, crises of all kinds. But will these obstacles deter us from experiencing what Jesus spoke of, or will they paint a portrait of his transformative work of grace in our lives? He designed us for meaningful relationship. Nothing less.

3

"THIS IS MEANINGFUL"

Mike Turk, executive pastor of organizational development at The MET, said:

As a staff and leaders, we understand the importance of having a clear mission statement that conveys why we exist as a church. It is also imperative that our mission statement be personally engaging—a call to action. In our first attempt at crafting a mission statement, we asked our staff to share words that they felt were true about who we were as a staff as well as words that we hoped the people in our church community would use to describe us. As a leadership team, we spent time individually and together wrestling with words and statements that embodied our mission as a church. With some help from a consultant, we created our first mission statement: "Leading others to follow Jesus and his essential methods for making disciples in meaningful relationship." While it was accurate, it wasn't necessarily crisp, compelling, or contagious. We needed a statement that could be easily carried and conveyed to others. This first attempt left people often stumbling over words or forgetting parts of the statement altogether.

After living with this mission statement for a couple of years, we recognized the mission statement itself wasn't sacred, and it was missing something. During a strategy meeting with our ministry leaders, we decided to put the mission statement on a flip chart on the wall, and we asked people what it was missing and what they would change about it. Some pointed out that it didn't come across as inviting, which ran counter to the disciple-making culture we were trying to build. Others soon joined in and shared that it didn't sound very relational or inclusive given that we want to reach people no matter where they are in their spiritual journey. As we shared thoughts and ideas, common themes began to emerge.

Earlier in the year, we had a sermon series that asked, "Lord, what are you inviting me into?" The thought that every circumstance could be viewed through the lens of "Lord, what are you inviting me into?" resonated at a heart level with much of our congregation and staff. We quickly determined that invitation had to be a part of the statement, and we didn't want to lose the focus on meaningful relationship. After an hour or so of passionate discussion, we had a new mission statement: "Inviting people into meaningful relationship with God and each other." It was crisp and contagious, a statement one could easily remember and share. It also served as a personal call to action for each of us as Christ followers and disciple makers—why we exist. The entire exercise of creating, evaluating, and refining was a powerful experience. We intentionally crafted and chose each word with the help of a creative consultant to make sure the statement represented who and what we wanted to be.

Let's break the mission statement down.

Inviting People

My heart is that we have a culture of invitation at The MET. Jesus himself always took someone with him: "Come and see," or "Come follow me." Throughout his ministry, he constantly invited people to come follow him. In our discipleship culture, we use the phrase "Take someone with you." The heart behind this phrase is to have the constant intention to involve others in what we are doing, whether by taking a meal to a grieving family, signing up for a Bible study class, or even on the drive to a weekly small group. In everything we do, we want to invite others to join us in both the big things and the little things.

Inviting People Into

We don't just invite people *to* something, but *into* something. There is a big difference in inviting people to church and inviting them into something that envelops and transforms. Inviting people *to* something is like a period on the end of a sentence. Inviting people *into* something is like a comma or an ellipsis. There is more to come! The word "into" suggests purpose and thoughtful intent behind the invitation. It changes the invitation from a simple investment of time and place to an investment of connection and relationship. It has movement. It has a continuum. It doesn't have a start time and an end time.

Inviting People into Meaningful Relationship

What are we inviting people *into?* It is relationship, but ponder the difference between a relationship and a "meaningful" relationship. That word is quite the game changer, isn't it? The definition of "meaningful" according to *Merriam-Webster Dictionary* is this: "full of meaning; significant."[2] The goal isn't just to have more relationships and more people in our lives; the goal is to have meaningful relationships. These are relationships that enrich our lives, sharpen us, and give us joy and comfort and support. These are relationships that matter.

Inviting People into Meaningful Relationship with God

Obviously, the priority of all relationships is one's relationship with God. There is no greater invitation that he extends to us or that we can extend to someone else. An important distinction must be made. The chasm between believing in God and having meaningful relationship with God is mammoth. For most of my Christian life, I was taught the importance of conversion. That moment someone walks from death to life and accepts Jesus Christ as Savior and Lord is by all definitions a meaningful change. But that meaningful event does not ensure a meaningful relationship. Just like in marriage how the wedding day is a meaningful event, but that event does not ensure a meaningful relationship. It takes time, proximity, and immense levels of intentionality, and it's no different with God.

Traditional church culture and the idol of religiosity can lend itself to lives unchanged by the power of Christ. But when relationship with God is meaningful—having honest conversations with him, obeying his commands, bearing fruit, living in community—it cannot be stagnant or unproductive. A meaningful relationship with God is characterized by joy and continual transformation. He is continually making us new!

Inviting People into Meaningful Relationship with God and Each Other

The truth that God, being relational himself, created a relational people to know and love him and to know and love each other, dumbfounds me. It leaves me in awe. God could've set it up any way he wanted, but he made the sanctification process happen best not only with him but also with other people. We see this from the garden in Genesis to the wedding feast in Revelation. We see it in the Ten Commandments and in the Great Commandment. We see it in the "one anothers" and in the fruit of the Spirit. The life of faith is fleshed out in community. Instead of asking the self-justifying question of "Who is my neighbor?" God invites us to become a loving neighbor to all. It's not the easy way, but isn't it beautiful?

"This Is Meaningful"

One evening Pastor Scott (teaching pastor at The MET) and I enjoyed some time hanging out with a few other men in our church. We talked about everything from baseball, to challenges with our kids and families, to our favorite wing sauce, and where we dreamed of going on vacation. None of the conversations would've been identified as life changing or memorable. But because of a continual investment in each other and a rhythm of proximity to one another and time shared, it was an emotionally safe place for men to be themselves. Even pastors need that!

We had just finished a series on our mission statement and marinated on the word "meaningful." As the men said their goodbyes, Scott looked at me and said, "*This* is meaningful." Yes, it was. Full of significance, full of purpose, full of meaning. What a gift.

4

FIGHT FOR RELATIONSHIP

Another critical cornerstone of this organization shift has been to keep relationship as the priority in times of disagreement or challenge. There have been days where organizationally we were at odds with someone, but we decided to fight for relationship above our agenda. This has been the silver bullet of the entire shift we have experienced. Most people fight for their opinion, their agenda, or the people they are representing. However, if you are going to lead change and tear down the existing church structure, you must be in relationship with those you lead, and then fight for that relationship to the very last breath.

Before I became senior pastor, I was on staff at The MET as the worship pastor. While serving in this role, I hired a longtime friend, Steven, as my associate. Steven had been a dear friend for many years, and we had traveled together and led worship. He came to The MET just as the discipleship culture was taking off. Steven became a devoted disciple maker, leading fruitful men's groups and launching disciples who made disciples. He was also just fun to be around. Working together was a dream come true!

He and his wife became some of the biggest supporters and prayer warriors during the church's transition. They had us over for dinner often to encourage us to keep pushing through in the difficult times. When I became senior pastor, they were over-joyed and fully supportive. As the organization began to align to relational discipleship, it demanded a commitment to align-ing people to mission and call. Just as I had been called to be a senior pastor, Steven moved toward a calling of shepherding stu-dents and their families.

As we sat on my back porch one afternoon, Steven asked a vulnerable question: "Tell me one thing that I don't want to hear." I answered his question with honesty and sincerity, and it led to a new level of vulnerability in our relationship. His cour-age to ask the question and my courage to give an honest, loving answer displayed the power of fighting for relationship in a very real and practical way. Even though we had been through rocky patches in our relationship before, he knew he could count on my love for him and that I would speak truth in love. He jokes today that perhaps I was a bit too honest that fateful day on that back porch, and maybe I was. God made us both practitioners of the art of relationship. And as I say over and over, the deepest relationships I have often come with the hardest conversations.

In the course of time there are situations that demand I lead *positionally*, but never without also leading *relationally*. For example, Jennifer and I sat across from Daren and his wife, Ashley, at a local bakery in Northwest Houston. Daren had been on staff for several years in various capacities. But in the end, I determined it best that we part ways. This is never an easy decision, especially with someone you love, but I believed it to be best for Daren and for The MET. This would challenge every ounce of relational equity we had built over previous years working together. With all the pain that had occurred, all the changes that had been made, this new culture we were attempting to build would be challenged. The commitment to meaningful relationship prevailed. Despite the end of Daren's time on staff, we asked a critical question: "Can we write a different story together?" This meant not running away from conflict but facing it head-on with a posture of reconciliation. All parties involved have done their part to forgive, speak truth in love, and keep an open posture to one another. I'm proud to say this couple is still at The MET. Daren works in our community but still teaches occasionally on the weekends, and Ashley is now on staff full-time. How is that for a new story?

Additionally, watching my own children adopt a relational discipleship culture has been eye-opening and one of my greatest joys. My girls have been immersed in this culture from their late elementary years on. The framework of relational discipleship to which we expose our next generation ministries sets the table for patterns of healthy relationships. My girls have learned what it means to be present in others' pain—not to fix or rescue—and to handle conflict with a sister in Christ in a biblically honoring way. It fosters a trust in the Holy Spirit to do the transformative work, while trusting our own mouths and words less and less.

The framework makes space for kids from all different walks of life to sit in a circle of safety among other teens, facilitated by two caring leaders. The fruit of this process in my children's lives leaves me dumbfounded regularly. Don't think for a moment that the commitment to relational discipleship will only manifest in your staff or in your own group. It will enter the fabric of your family as well.

Another example of fighting for relationship involved Pastor Scott, whom I referenced earlier. He had been suddenly fired by our church's previous leadership. Scott then moved to Folsom, California, near Sacramento, and he started a traveling and speaking ministry, teaching in various churches around the country. We stayed in touch periodically and always dreamed of getting to do ministry together again at some point, but Texas was off Scott's radar as a potential landing spot considering all that had happened.

One day, I felt God speaking to me about the possibility of helping restore the relationship our church had with Scott. He had been wounded deeply, and as the new senior pastor, I now had the opportunity to extend a hand for purposes of restoration. I and our church had deeply loved Scott. He had been the face that I initially connected with in my journey to The MET. He had made the initial invitation as well as the offer for me to come on staff as worship pastor.

I gave Scott a call. "Would you be willing to come back to The MET, experience the culture of relationship here, preach on a weekend, and let us love on you again?"

There was definite reluctance there.

"Would you be willing to think about it?" I asked.

He eventually agreed. When I saw him before he went on the stage, his palms were sweaty. Our team prayed over him. But after he spoke for a few minutes, the anxiety lifted from him. People encouraged him, gladly welcomed him back, and were thrilled with the church being in relationship with Scott once again. "I can't tell you how thankful I am," he said later over a meal. Scott continued to fly in periodically and teach for us on various weekends, and the relationship moved from simply being restored to a new calling.

Scott was on his own journey with God. "I think God is calling me and my family back into full-time local church ministry," he told me. In my heart, I knew God was calling Scott to join us at The MET. What a redemptive story, an incredible wink from God. But Texas wasn't necessarily top on his list as he searched out what God was asking him to do. I didn't know where he would end up, but I asked God to place him somewhere he could thrive and be all God was calling him to be.

God was in it every step of the way. Later, I called and asked Scott to prayerfully consider coming on staff at The MET. Scott responded, "We have received opportunities from larger churches, even with more money, but the opportunity to do ministry alongside you and the culture of relationship that I have experienced at The MET is where God is leading. And let's not forget the cost of living in Texas! We are headed to Houston!"

It was incredible to see the power of fighting for restored relationship. Scott currently serves on our executive leadership team. He leads our teaching ministry and our marketing and communication department. He is a disciple maker. It is just another reminder that God can heal any relationship if we give him access to it and then fight for it with everything we've got.

This was one of the biggest disciplines I had to personally commit myself to. I don't love conflict. Early on as the senior pastor, I often felt as if a conflict was an employee not being willing to follow my leadership. It threatened me. Why? Because I'm the leader, and I believed where I led people, they needed to go. Leadership is often threatened where relationship is birthed. Good leaders do the hard work of taking off their positional hat often, laying down their authority, and humbling themselves. Leaders, we must be in relationship with those we lead if we are going to fight for it. We must allow others to speak freely, engage their interests, and stay fully present in meetings even when their strategy differs from our own.

As we transitioned our church to a relational discipleship model, I knew it was going to have to begin with me and my style of leadership. I couldn't lead positionally and demand relational alignment. I had to fight for the main thing: meaningful relationship. I had to decide that above all agendas and plans for future development, I was going to have to be willing to know and be known by my staff and their families.

The conviction of fighting for relationship is a value of mine to my core, but at times, I have also thought it would cost me everything. Experiencing rejection while maintaining an open posture toward someone is indescribable. In this way, I have truly learned to identify with the sufferings of Christ. I identify with the heart of my Savior when someone with whom I have done life is no longer near me. As David said: "For it is not an enemy who taunts me—then I could bear it; it is not an adversary who deals insolently with me—then I could hide from him. But it is you, a man, my equal, my companion, my familiar friend. We used to take sweet counsel together; within God's house we walked in the throng" (Ps. 55:12–13, ESV).

We are not alone, friends, when we seek to live out Jesus' model and it becomes hurtful and hard. This is when we experience the sweetest intimacy with the Savior and a greater understanding of what he experienced with those he walked with. Because of the grace he shows me, I can show grace to others.

Barriers to Fighting for Relationship

Fighting for relationship is easier said than done. It forces relational development of epic proportions. Because of its extreme challenges, it comes with barriers that prevent so many from ever experiencing its fruit.

Soul Health. Fighting for relationship demands constant awareness of my spiritual and emotional health. I have not always approached soul health with the vigilance I do today, but I wish I had. You will be hamstrung in your ability to experience this shift personally, let alone leading the shift in your organization, if you fail to care deeply for your soul. The hurts and hangups that we stumble into—and revisit frequently—can fester into relational carnage. They must be attended to with care and attention. No leader who is unaware of their tendencies in this area can grow to their full potential. There must be awareness and commitment to rewiring of their thinking.

Also, let us not overlook our own internal growth and discipleship for the sake of ministry outcomes outside of us. I never again want to be a part of a ministry that cares more about external goals than internal health. No more ignoring the fruit of our own lives, leaving hurt and offended people in the wake of our leadership. As James says, "It ought not to be so" (James 3:10, ESV).

People. Jesus' model of loving people unconditionally, as well as so many admonishments in the epistles, helps us see the prioritization of loving people as we go through life. Being a Christian has been relegated to church attendance and moral behavior, and we have neglected careful examination of our interaction with every "neighbor" in our lives—starting with those with whom we live.

Paul says in Galatians 5 that the flesh and spirit are at war, the manifestation of which is all kinds of sin and division. In that same chapter, he reminds us of what it is to love our neighbor and avoid the result of destroyed relationship if we continue to "bite and devour." The "bite and devour" mentality does not allow the Spirit to bear the stunning fruit only born out of biblical relationship.

Remember, meaningful relationship is forged in the fire of conflict. If your heart is to love, then conflict can be the foundation and a catalyst for a deeper relationship with those you lead.

Shark Tank Mentality. I love watching *Shark Tank.* The entrepreneurial spirit—seeing men and women bring their ideas to life in hopes of landing a deal that will propel them into future wealth, fame, and success—inspires me. Some of those principles have invaded the modern-day church, which is alarming if you think about it. Church culture might say that there are certain skills leaders must possess, certain programs they must have, certain financial numbers they must hit, and certain attendance numbers they must attain all in hopes of being pre-sented on the nation's "fastest-growing churches in America" list. But all this just gets in the way of knowing and being known by others.

We cannot try to live invincibly when Jesus calls us to live vulnerably. We may not want to be Mr. Wonderful, but are we striving to lead more like our favorite mega-church pastor or more like Jesus? He said the greatest among us is the servant of all—laying one's life down, admitting mistakes, and leading with vulnerability. Are we mimicking a leader's public image to the neglect of the private life it takes to sustain such success? If so, we are misguided. And Jesus' church suffers in the process.

High-profile leaders fall prey to their church's "success" at alarming rates. When those we lead don't truly know us, we're isolated. When we are isolated, we're not accountable. When we are not accountable, we lose sight of ourselves, and the end of our fruitful ministry approaches quickly.

Isolation. It's easy for leaders not to see themselves—and their situations—clearly. In 2 Samuel 12, we find the story of Nathan confronting David about his sin:

> The LORD sent Nathan to David. When he came to him, he said, "There were two men in a certain town, one rich and the other poor. The rich man had a very large number of sheep and cattle, but the poor man had nothing except one little ewe lamb he had bought. He raised it, and it grew up with him and his children. It shared his food, drank from his cup and even slept in his arms. It was like a daughter to him.

"Now a traveler came to the rich man, but the rich man
refrained from taking one of his own sheep or cattle to
prepare a meal for the traveler who had come to him.
Instead, he took the ewe lamb that belonged to the poor
man and prepared it for the one who had come to him."

David burned with anger against the man and said to
Nathan, "As surely as the LORD lives, the man who did
this must die! He must pay for that lamb four times over,
because he did such a thing and had no pity."

Then Nathan said to David, "You are the man! This is
what the LORD, the God of Israel, says: 'I anointed you
king over Israel, and I delivered you from the hand of Saul.
I gave your master's house to you, and your master's wives
into your arms. I gave you all Israel and Judah. And if all
this had been too little, I would have given you even more.
Why did you despise the word of the LORD by doing what
is evil in his eyes?" . . .

Then David said to Nathan, "I have sinned against the
LORD." (2 Sam. 12:1–9, 13)

David had deceived himself into thinking he was leading well,
taking up the cause of someone who could not defend himself.
But his power and lack of accountability left him deeply flawed.
No one dared confront him about his sin with Bathsheba. It
took great courage for Nathan to confront David about what
he had done, especially when David had the power to kill him.
But because of Nathan's boldness, David was able to heed his

warning, humble himself, and turn from his wicked ways. As leaders, we need to humble ourselves and see ourselves for what we really are. Our identity must be anchored in God's declaration of us as his children.

Bridges to Fighting for Relationship

As difficult as it is to learn the skill of fighting for relationship, some key practices can ensure that you are on the right track.

Abiding in Christ. When we build our identities on the shaky foundation of how many people are in a pew or how many attend the programs we run on Sunday mornings, we will always find ourselves trying to achieve success on our own merits. John 15:4–6 says:

> Remain in me, as I also remain in you. No branch can bear fruit by itself; it must remain in the vine. Neither can you bear fruit unless you remain in me. I am the vine; you are the branches. If you remain in me and I in you, you will bear much fruit; apart from me you can do nothing. If you do not remain in me, you are like a branch that is thrown away and withers; such branches are picked up, thrown into the fire and burned.

There are so many things we commit our lives to as leaders. The culture of our teams, the vision we are preparing to cast, the funds we need to raise—you fill in the blank. But Jesus' words ring true in my soul again: "Apart from me you can do nothing." We are not called to lead first; rather, we are called to follow first. We must lay our agendas, our abilities, and our attention to things other than Jesus aside in order to pick up the relationship with him as the top priority.

J. D. Greear, in his book *Gaining by Losing*, says: "When Christ calls any of us to follow him—whether he is speaking to us as individuals, or to our churches and ministries—he bids us, 'Come and die.' It is not through our success that God saves the world, but through our *sacrifice*. He calls us first to an altar, not a platform."[3] The key to a better model of discipleship is dying to ourselves so we can plant life into those whom God has entrusted us to lead. When we shed the skin of our former selves, we take on the appearance of our new selves in Christ. When we focus on others instead of ourselves and stop allowing our egos to be in charge, we can enter into real relationship with God, ourselves, and then with others. We can see people without loving people, but we can't love people without seeing people. We can't love others if we don't know how to love ourselves. We must be identified *with* Christ so we can be *in* relationship with Christ.

Proximity to People. When I think of the proximity that Jesus chose to live in with people—those who hurt him, those who disappointed him, those who didn't believe him—I am in awe of his staying close despite the impending emotional pain and sting of rejection. I think of his gentle example in washing the feet of Judas at the Last Supper, of sharing the cup with him, all while knowing the betrayal that would take place just a few hours later. I think of his tenderness and compassion toward the city of Jerusalem, as he looked out over the city that rejected the very person who would give them peace. He knew the voices that cried, "Hosanna!" would be the same ones to cry, "Crucify him!" a few days later. I think of his investment in the Twelve and the evidence of his astonishment when they still gravitated toward fear, self-promotion, and self-protection despite all he had modeled and given in those three years. He stayed close both physically and emotionally.

If that's not fighting for relationship, I don't know what is!

5

THE GIFT
OF WITH

Our world is loud. News channels, social media feeds, and even sporting events bombard us with noise. What's more, we have so much easy access to noise that we miss out on the gift of solitude and the practice of being fully present with the people in our lives. Most importantly, we miss out on being fully present with Jesus.

After I had served ten years at The MET (five years as senior pastor), my elders approached me about taking a sabbatical. At first, I tried to negotiate. "Can't it just be three or four weeks?" I bargained. But after they prayed, they lovingly came to me and said it should be at least six weeks for me to truly experience the gift of rest and true Sabbath. I reluctantly agreed.

The elders asked me to have a plan in place for my Sabbath. They wanted me to answer key questions before I entered this rest period. Some of the questions they asked were:

- What are you going to read while you are gone?
- Where are you going to go? Why?
- Whom will you go see and whom will you take with you? Why?

It wasn't difficult for me to think through who was going to go with me because I wanted to spend time with my wife and two daughters. The time didn't have to be super spiritual; rather, I just wanted to be present in the moment without the distraction of the outside noises I lived with every day. But I also knew I wanted to carve out significant time to spend in solitude with God. I had never done that before.

I didn't know how my sabbatical would play out. I just knew I needed a break, and this was it. But I was specifically asked to spend time alone with God—just me and God. I'm an extrovert by nature. As I get older, I've become more introverted, but this was going to be a challenge for sure. The first couple of hours of solitude for an extrovert is no big deal. After that, you might as well gouge my eyes out with an ice pick! *Whom do I talk to? Whom can I call? It's too quiet!*

For a portion of my travel, I drove from Oklahoma City, where I had dropped my kids off with their grandparents, to Santa Fe, New Mexico. I had a new cell phone number, with no access to my contact list, no access to email, and no podcasts. The first leg of my trip was from Oklahoma City to Amarillo. (I can hear you singing George Strait. Don't pretend you're not!) It was just me and the open road for four hours. At first, I simply took in the surroundings. Hot air hit me in the face as I rolled down the window and listened to the cadence of the tires as they touched the road. Those were all sounds I had previously drowned out by turning on the radio or talking to someone on the phone.

Then I began to hear sounds I hadn't paid attention to before. The rumbles of thunder from a storm in the distance. The *whoosh* of tires on a car as it accelerated past me. I had taken these sounds for granted because of my tendency to become easily distracted, and now they were the sole focus of my attention. That's when the busyness began to slow down, and my mind truly began to embrace this thing called the Sabbath.

When we consider the Sabbath, we talk about rest. Rest is a natural part of the creation account, as if God wants us to live from a place of rest, not simply work toward rest. I heard God whisper something during my time with him: "Matt, you are not a human doing. You are a human being." I had lost the art of *being* because I was so busy *doing*. It's an important reality we all must face—the world doesn't fall apart because I stop doing things. But if I quit being, I lose both my identity and my connection with this world.

My life is not a gift to this world; it's a gift to me. I had to adjust my attitude from being busy to recognizing that being on this earth for this time, for this season, and for this generation is a privilege. If my being falls apart, everything else falls apart too. This principle defined and underscored my entire sabbatical experience.

With God

The next day, I got up early, drove four more hours, and arrived in Santa Fe, New Mexico. I stayed in a friend's home, about 7,500 feet up in the mountains. Each morning, I'd get up, read my Bible, do some extrabiblical reading as well, then head up the hill for some hiking. One morning, I looked out toward the mountains and didn't see a cloud in the sky. The sun was at my back, and I felt the Holy Spirit ask me a tough question: "Who are you when all that stuff fades away?"

I sat quietly, and then responded in my heart, *I have value, but the role of pastor doesn't make me the most valuable voice in the room.* Think about it this way: when we are in the presence of the president or some other powerful figure, and they speak, everyone else in the room gets quiet, allowing the president's voice to be the most prominent voice in the room.

But I wasn't living that way with God.

I had to remind myself of a few key truths:

- I'm a son of God.
- I'm not the most prominent figure in God's story.
- I'm here for the purposes and plans of the one who created me.
- I have nowhere to be but with him.
- I have nothing God wants from me.
- But I do have things God wants for me.

I had to wrestle with those realities and just be present with him. That in and of itself was a challenge. I had come into this time of solitude with big expectations! But those expectations had to take a back seat to God's purposes for me in the quiet moments. And believe me, it was quiet. But I wanted to experience the voice of God and know that we were in this together.

On the second day, I asked God directly, "Are you even with me in this moment in time? I just want to know that you're here. Would you show me that you are with me?" A little while later I came down out of the mountains and felt tired, so I went back to my room. I lay down on the couch and scrolled through movie titles on TV and looked for something to watch. Based on what I had already watched, the TV gave me some recommendations. My love of baseball was evident from the suggested titles. It recommended the movie *Talent for the Game* that was released in 1991. Looking for something to fall asleep to, I thought, *This is perfect*. I pressed play, and then waited to be lulled to sleep.

Instead, the Lord spoke.

The movie is about a scout about to lose his job unless he lands a super-talented prospect. He has one lead, a young man playing high school baseball in the Palouse hills. This scout hops in his red convertible with the top down and travels with his wife to North Idaho. My interest was piqued to say the least. I had finished high school and my first year of college in the Palouse hills of Idaho also! After my grade school years, my parents had moved us there from the Chicago suburbs.

During this couple's drive through the beautiful countryside, the car breaks down, and they tow it into the small town of Genesee, Idaho. The mechanic working on their car happens to be the father of the boy whom the scout hopes to find. As they discuss the potential future of the young player, the camera pans across a baseball field . . . and a collision of worlds happened for me personally.

I quickly realized that the film depicted the same baseball field where I had played high school baseball. Back then I had attended a private school, and the school didn't have the resources for baseball or football teams. Instead, it had a co-op with a small public high school in—you guessed it—Genesee, Idaho. I had driven to that same baseball field and practiced there every day.

In that moment, the Lord looked deep into my soul and winked. It was as if he said, "I've got you. And, Matt, I *am* with you." In this moment, I realized a simple yet profound truth: I am never alone.

Matthew 28 has a profound truth at the end of the Great Commission that now gripped me with a fresh new perspective: "And surely, I am with you always, to the very end of the age." I had understood the Great Commission in the context of missional living, the going and making of disciples. But knowing that he is with me always, no matter what I am doing, is a different posture. The drama I face, the friends who mistreat me, the temptations I deal with, the problems that I face that generations before me didn't have to face—God is always with me. In social media language, I am "followed" by Christ himself!

Being with people should be different than just knowing they are there. When we are with people, we experience their unique perspectives. At times, some of those preferences even become our own! It is the same with God. When we experience God's presence, His will becomes our will. But we must do our part. Earlier on that mountain, I hadn't heard him. I had prayed and asked God to answer my requests, but I hadn't paid attention to what God wanted. He had been there all along. I just hadn't listened.

Listening Journal

I had to heighten my awareness of who God was. I needed to listen to him more than I had been. I needed to allow his perspectives and preferences to permeate my life. Often, though, it took a crisis to land me on my knees. I asked God to do mega miracles for me in faith, but often I didn't obey him in the small things that he had made abundantly clear. What did I need to do to embrace the gift of "with"?

Before I left for sabbatical, I had started writing a new journal, but not like the ordinary journals I had always done. I called it a "listening journal." Anytime I talked to someone and felt the conversation pertained to me and my situation, I wrote it down. If I believed it applied directly to me, I simply took out a pen and asked, "Can I write this down?" I wrote down the quote, and then put the person's name next to it.

For example, in my small group on a Monday evening my friend Chris said, "Don't find your identity in the accomplishments of your kids." To me, that was profound and spoke directly to my heart. Writing these quotes and phrases down not only helps me remember them, but God also continues to remind me of them when I make room to be more aware of him in my everyday life. That genuine curiosity, the intentional listening for the whisper of the Holy Spirit in every circumstance, has revolutionized my devotional life, my leadership strategies, and my heart for people. And I listen differently because of my experience.

With Others

I asked Jason, a newcomer to my small group, if I could ride with him during his workday. I knew that time and proximity would be critical for us to develop a real, meaningful relationship. Jason said yes, but I could hear the hesitancy in his voice. There was something he could use my help with: a delivery he had to make to the southern part of the city. It would be an hour drive there and back, plus a load/unload situation, along with several stops at various vendors on the way back.

I hopped into his pickup truck early that morning; we grabbed some coffee, put some worship music on, and hit the Houston traffic. Small talk ensued, phones rang, emails were sent. I put my earbuds in my ear, made some calls as he drove, and he put in a full workday. Some of our conversations during our downtime were deep and meaningful about various aspects of life; other times, we didn't talk at all. I came with no agenda but simply to get to know Jason, to be with him, and to trust the process of building a relationship with someone in whom I saw amazing leadership potential. He was new to the faith, and I was mesmerized by his questions, his insight, and the thought process he engaged as his faith deepened and grew.

As our relationship developed over time, Jason began to ask more and more questions about faith, the church, and the mission of the church. He developed new habits and gained new circles of friends. It was just amazing to see God change his heart and use him to change mine as well.

I had met Jason through Christian, a new staff member at our church, who had invited Jason to our men's small group. Jason often asked questions until late in the evening as the group dissipated. We stood out by the truck for hours sometimes, just enjoying the gift of being together and listening as the Holy Spirit instructed, taught, encouraged, and equipped. As I watched him grow, I realized it wasn't me teaching him theology in a classroom that would grow him or would ultimately make him a leader. Rather, it was his desire for growth. Jason was willing to do his part. I had to do my part, and God always does his part.

True discipleship happens within the context of meaningful relationships. These relationships don't happen overnight, nor do they happen with a quick exchange on a Sunday morning. Real growth begins when I live out my own commitment to move from transactional to meaningful. Jason made the same commitment, and God did all the teaching and instruction. To this day, this remains one of my favorite things in my life as a disciple: surrendering my heart to what God is doing in someone's life and staying faithful to engage and participate. The outcome always astounds me.

Jason was free to ask any questions that were on his heart. He even had moments when he shared his doubts about the faith. He didn't have a strong Bible knowledge at the time, although that has grown as he has grown. No one judged him when he asked questions; we loved and accepted him just as he was. We didn't expect him to have it all together; we just wanted him to come wanting Jesus. Jason now serves as an elder in our church.

Learn to value the "gift of with." It will change your leadership.

Obstacles to the Gift of With

As you learn to value the "gift of with," you will feel the tension build. The call to slow down and treasure each moment is often met with resistance on all sides. In these moments remember the battle is worth every second of the fight. There are obstacles to living this way, most of which reside in the inner self.

Ego. As I vowed to be present with God in every facet of life, I had to manage one big hindrance differently: my ego. I had to tell my ego it wasn't in charge of my life. All the leadership titles I have assumed in life—husband, father, pastor—are all subordinate to God. I'm a follower first, a leader second. I realized I needed to let go of offenses and die to the need to be affirmed, approved of, and exalted in every situation. I didn't need to be known by the world. God made the world, and I am known by God. I had to surrender my will to the will of Jesus. My ego had to take a back seat. It's an everyday battle, but well worth fighting. I must daily surrender to the "gift of with."

Motives. To enter into meaningful relationship with God, I had to analyze my motives. I'd love to say I'm always motivated by the gospel. Sometimes I am, but other times, when my ego is in the way, I want to win more than I want to be present with him. I live with a divided heart—part of me wants to live for Jesus, and the other part wants to be seen as a success. When my ego is in check, then my motives can be examined. When my motives are pure, I can live as a person with integrity and an authentic example of who God made me to be.

We must be careful here. Often, when we talk to people and they say something that affirms our motives, we easily believe that is God affirming us. Leaders, please pay attention: all affirmation is not God's affirmation. The abundant use of "God told me" language renders spiritual leaders less and less trustworthy. I have been hurt deeply by fellow leaders who told me they "heard from God" when in fact they heard from their own egos and motives. We must also confirm the voice in our hearts and heads through prayer, the Word of God, other God followers, and circumstances. It is critical. When we claim to hear from God but haven't truly heard from him, we are on a slippery slope, and our own agendas quickly crowd out his whisper.

What if we came to God with no ulterior motives, no hidden agendas, no hunger for success? What if instead we fully surrender ourselves to him and enter his presence with nothing else than the desire to be with him? As we establish this as a pattern of our time with God, it also seeps into our time with others. Spending time with and being fully present with the people in my life has proven to be of far greater value than any agenda items that need to be checked off a proverbial list. Yes, at times some tasks need to get done. But bringing in a fresh lens of "with" will significantly strengthen connections with those with whom we have relationship. I promise.

Part 2

ORGANIZATIONAL ALIGNMENT

6

THE ENGINE
OF THE LOCAL
CHURCH

A s I mentioned earlier, the concept of relational discipleship
had collided with our church leadership at their first DiscipleShift training in Post Falls, Idaho, at Real Life Ministries.
The seeds of relational discipleship had been planted, and now
the leadership had to wrestle with what they had experienced.

The spring that I first came to The MET, I also partook in
the training. After I experienced relational discipleship, I didn't
want anything else. I realized it had been elusive in my ministry life, and even in my personal discipleship. I was inspired
and transformed but overwhelmed at the thought of tearing
down a twenty-year-old ministry framework and rebuilding it

around Matthew 4:19: "Follow me, and I will make you fishers of men" (ESV).

Getting that DNA to permeate every corner of that church was a daunting task. The leaders of the church jumped in personally to the best of their abilities and began to start small groups. The rest of the church carried on as usual for that season until we had traction.

A couple of years later, I was at a Starbucks with a fellow pastor one morning, wrestling through some of these topics, when I grabbed a napkin and started drawing.

If growing a disciple of Jesus to full maturity in Christ was the goal, and relationship was the means, what other elements were critical to aiding people in their spiritual pursuits? What ministries must surface, and what other ministries must be put to pasture? The center of the target was clear, but I began categorizing current and future ministry offerings around it and assessing the themes. Within two weeks, I had whiteboarded what we now refer to as the Engine of the Local Church.

THE ENGINE OF THE LOCAL CHURCH

Inviting people into meaningful relationship with God and each other

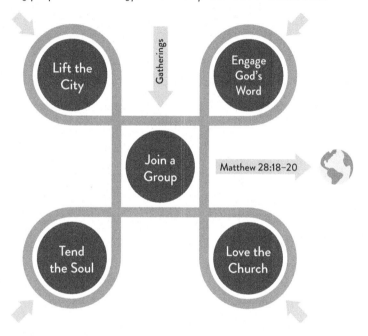

As you can see, it's a simple drawing but has been one of the single greatest tools for church alignment we've experienced. What began as an assessment of the battles we would face as we moved toward our new vision became an incredibly insightful revelation. God continues to use this tool in powerful ways each time we share it with others.

Think of it this way: within each circle of the engine are elements of spiritual need. As a person intentionally engages each element of the engine, spiritual growth and maturity begin to form at a rapid pace. The critical idea, however, is that a disciple engages *each* element.

Let's look at each element specifically.

Join a Group

We must live in relationship with one another. This is the center of the mark. This is what we've talked about throughout the pages of this book and what we invite the world *into*, the sharing of life. Paul said in 1 Thessalonians 2:8: "So we cared for you. Because we loved you so much, we were delighted to share with you not only the gospel of God but our lives as well." The invitation is not simply to conversion but also into a relationship with God. At the same time, spending time with his people is critical to learning how to live out the new life in Christ. We must engage the people of God to mature in our faith. We cannot have a meaningful relationship with God without being committed to his people.

Engage God's Word

The study of God's Word is an essential part of a healthy disciple. Traditional Bible studies or Sunday school hadn't produced the transforming fruit I hoped. It transferred knowledge and connected and cared for people, but I didn't see an interaction with Scripture in a way that reproduced disciple makers. No pathway for reproducing was evident. The Sunday school classes didn't model consistent growth and often became "holy huddles," with some classes having gathered consistently for decades.

As I assessed this, small groups had already launched, and there was tension between the small groups and Sunday school classes. The complaint of the classes was that the groups didn't go "deep enough" into the Scripture and ran the risk of being "errant" as lay people facilitated those groups through stories adapted from the Scripture. The obvious critique of the class model was it didn't reproduce disciple-making disciples.

The critical understanding is that both are essential to a vibrant, growing disciple—a relational small group where one fleshes out the realities of God's Word in their everyday lives as well as a setting for engaging God's Word to grow in knowledge and reverence for the Bible. In both cases, one without the other falls short.

Love the Church

Giving financially and supporting the bride with spiritual gifts and acts of service are great indicators for consistent growth. It should be obvious to God and others that everything we possess, whether it is time, money, or gifts, is being invested into God's kingdom. A growing disciple of Jesus is willing to do inconvenient things for the cause of Christ.

We need to consider something here. Many people love to serve and to give generously of time and treasure, but unfortunately it stops there. They slip in and out of the worship services on Sunday mornings without ever truly being connected to the body of Christ. We should pay close attention to the model in Acts 2. The brothers and sisters in that local community took care of one another. They sold what they had and sacrificially gave of themselves for one another.

We live in a more cause-oriented generation than ever before. But for a disciple of Jesus, it's not about a social cause but about Jesus' church. The bride of Christ is the cause Jesus gave his life to save. The more we love Jesus' church in how we prioritize giving and serving, then what matters to God will matter to us more.

Tend the Soul

When Jesus calls us to love one another as we love ourselves, we see that neglecting the care for oneself hinders the ability to love others well. All of us have not elevated this component appropriately—me included—and have seen and experienced the effects of it. Yet the pull to selfless living coupled with the confines of our human capabilities is vital in our awareness as a disciple maker. We must see ourselves as God sees us, working through the wounding pain of circumstances, and, ironically, the pain that we experience in relationships throughout life.

At its core, loving oneself, tending the soul, is a commitment to healing. We all need healing. That understanding and the humility to engage it are necessary to grow in our relationship with Jesus.

Lift the City

Jeremiah spoke of the captivity of God's people in Babylon. Even in their captivity, the people received a word from the Lord through the prophet. They were to "seek the welfare of the city" (Jer. 29:7, ESV) and look on it with compassion. Compassion ministries represent the relationship to the "neighbors" of the church. Loving them well means we have our collective "chin up," looking outward with the realization that the community doesn't exist to come to church; rather, the church exists to go to the community. Being others-focused is one of the primary ways we grow in Christ. It demands that we consider others' needs above our own. It means that we not only know what we believe but also why we believe it.

The Great Commission (Matthew 28:18–20)

One of the challenges I saw initially was where missions fit into the engine. Missions work was traditionally associated with giving money to missionaries or people taking mission trips to various places nationally or internationally. After our church let go of what traditional "missions work" looked like, we saw the entire picture as one of mission. As a disciple lives a life moving through each component of the engine of the local church, spiritual growth and maturity begin to take place. Missions then is not simply giving financial aid to those who are in other parts of the country or the world. Instead, it is the making and sending of disciple makers as well as equipping and encouraging other disciple-making churches. Not only are we to make and send disciples of Jesus personally, but we also are to disciple other churches locally, nationally, and internationally. It is a practice that we celebrate often.

This passion needs to be reawakened in the hearts of church leaders around the world. There is too much competition and not enough support. There is too much debate and not enough sacrifice. The social agenda of our nation has rendered us "a-missional," and it shows in the data as well as in the lack of relational intuition and integrity in our members. Missions is simple: reproduce other disciples and other disciple-making churches.

Gathering

After looking at what I had sketched, I was alarmed to see that after sixteen years of ministry as a worship pastor, I didn't even have Sunday morning services represented on this diagram. It shocked me as I examined it. I would say as much as 80 percent of any given church's resources and energies center on what is done on Sunday morning. It is the main entry point for most people, and unfortunately, often becomes their final destination.

As I reexamined the drawing, I added "gathering" as a funnel to the top of the engine. It is the widest, most welcoming door for many, but we don't want people to stop there. The essential component of the engine is movement. Though the gathering is essential, if it's the primary focus, it falls short of drawing people to the kind of transformation that happens in relational environments week in and week out.

Each element of the engine can be an entry point, but it takes the entire engine to call people into meaningful relationship with God and each other.

All in Love

As I presented the engine early on, an older church member, David, pulled me aside. "Matt, love holds that whole thing together. If we don't love each other, it just falls apart!"

David had hit the nail on the head. As I pondered what he said, the Holy Spirit led me to consider the effects of those pieces without love, and I found a perfect lens for the engine in

1 Corinthians 13. Remember, the apostle Paul didn't write this chapter for the first wedding he performed. He didn't even write it for that purpose; he wrote it to a local church. And it is a perfect lens for life.

Discover how it overlays on the parts of the engine:

> If I speak in the tongues of men or of angels, but do not have love, I am a resounding gong or a clanging cymbal. If I have the gift of prophecy and can fathom all mysteries and knowledge, and if I have a faith that can move the mountains, but do not have love, I am nothing. If I give all I possess to the poor and give over my body to hardship that I may boast, but do not have love, I gain nothing. (1 Cor. 13:1–3)

Without love and without movement in the process of discipleship, we become stagnant as well as annoying and unfruitful. Knowledge without love puffs up. Serving without love leads to burnout and gains nothing. Camping out in recovery ministries for endless seasons of ministry trades one codependency for another. Caring for self to the neglect of loving others leaves us introspective and self-absorbed. This passage beautifully shows us the pitfalls of amazingly good things gone terribly wrong without love. Without love, the spiritual needle does not move.

Paul then writes:

> Love is patient, love is kind. It does not envy, it does not boast, it is not proud. It does not dishonor others, it is not self-seeking, it is not easily angered, it keeps no record of wrongs. Love does not delight in evil but rejoices with

the truth. It always protects, always trusts, always hopes, always perseveres. Love never fails. (1 Cor. 13:4–8a)

So love is what ties it all together. John 13:35 says, "By this everyone will know that you are my disciples, if you love one another." It is not our ministry programming that displays who we follow, nor is it the size of our platform that shows our maturity in Christ. It is the way we love each other. It is how we love each other in disputes and disagreements. Love is the critical component to being a disciple and making disciples.

Paul next talks about what stays and what passes away. He speaks of what is childish and what is mature. He affirms the fact that we see in a glass darkly now, but then we will see clearly, face-to-face. The one who fully knows us now is our Lord and Savior, Jesus Christ. And either when we pass from this life or when he comes to take us home, we will know him fully.

An echo of being fully known by our Savior is stepping toward being fully known on this earth. What if we were part of building discipleship cultures that created incubators for people to feel safe enough to be known in an atmosphere of love as they move toward intimacy with Christ and with others?

I left a thriving worship ministry with connections, stages, and popularity that many pastors might envy. Yet I left it for the mission. After my eyes were opened to the mission, I couldn't go back to ministry as I knew it. Tears sting my eyes as I type this. I plead with you to consider doing church differently—a way that ministers to your soul and immerses you in discipleship culture that is messy, hard, painful, yet abundantly fruitful.

7

TEARING DOWN THE HIGH PLACES: WHAT IS A HIGH PLACE?

Not only did each leader at The MET have to align their heart and mind to Jesus' methods, but as we persisted in the call to lead a church in this direction, it was evident that many of the ministries we had put in place over the years must transition as well. Relationship had to be the center of everything as the church moved forward. The entire organization needed to align to relational discipleship. As we lead, we mustn't live within one theological understanding while leading within another.

Fast forward a few years later, and relational discipleship began to take hold. We had small groups that multiplied. We launched leadership training to train new leaders and multiply groups. We communicated our new language from the stage, and it became more common among our staff and congregation. Significant change took place. The ship had sailed, and it was so exciting to be a part—both personally and corporately. Ministry as I had known it was gone.

When our senior pastor of nearly twenty years transitioned out, the leadership of the church temporarily fell to the lead team and me. I saw the need for more of this transformation to permeate all aspects of the church. I was determined that we weren't going to "play church" in one facet and "do relational discipleship" in another. Alignment was critical for this to be sustained. But I couldn't see how it would encapsulate all the essential functions and ministries of the church and sync together. Relational discipleship was supposed to synergize and fuel all aspects of the church, but what did that look like?

Any leader worth their salt recognizes the need for organizational alignment. If the various parts of the organization we lead are aimed in different directions, we spend way too much time cleaning up messes that are anything but small. What's more, the longer an organization exists, the more propensity it has to pick up pseudo-alignment strategies from various leaders (staff or otherwise) and sit on those strategies until Jesus returns. It is why leading change is so difficult. It's why some leaders plant churches rather than lead churches to shift. It takes grit to plant a church, but it also takes a different kind of grit to make a major organizational shift. This "grind it out" mentality encompasses more than just staying power to keep moving forward. It requires a determination to advance against established patterns, beliefs, rhythms, and strongholds. It takes relational grit. We must be willing to go through the torture of conflict, disagreements, hurt feelings, people leaving the church. That separation is a heavy one—one that I don't even believe we were created to experience, which is why it is so difficult to navigate. So many sacred cows live in the pastures of tenured organizations. Ours were top programs that began with incredible motivations but were stagnant in their approach as the culture shifted. They were memories of the good ol' days. And as we looked at the organization holistically, we recognized that we needed to make a few changes immediately to align our organization to our mission.

I am a fairly relational guy, fun-loving, athletic, and competitive—for the most part I like a good challenge. But I must confess that I experienced new levels of grief, frustration, and anger as we began this process. Alignment to a new mission, and ultimately a new focus, doesn't come cheap. It is extremely relationally expensive, all in the name of building relationships. Ironic, isn't it?

At the heart of the matter was our elders and leadership team wanting to blaze a new path forward, standing on the shoulders of those who had gone before us. They had taken this church through their share of campaigns and visionary moments, and now it was our turn. Burn the ships! Let's go!

Here's the reality: after a church is established with any sense of history or tradition, you as a leader are standing at what seems like the base of Mount Everest. At almost every turn, change-management and deconstruction require a self-emptying dependence on the Lord. It is sweat and tears, but more than that, it's care, love, and patience amid a deep desire to see progress in the organization. The tension feels like it will pull you apart at times. It did me.

People are creatures of habit and comfort, and while we all know that to be true, the price we as leaders must pay to lead people through the waters of change is steep. Samuel R. Chand once said:

> Leadership that doesn't produce pain is either in a short season of unusual blessing or it isn't really making a difference. . . . When leaders in any field take the risk of moving individuals and organizations from one stage to another—from stagnation to effectiveness or from success to significance—they inevitably encounter confusion, passivity, and outright resistance from those they're trying to lead.[4]

Determining that relational discipleship would be at the center of our church's DNA meant all ministries had to be examined with a microscope, the budget had to be combed through, and all our programming had to be challenged. Everything ranging from our organizational chart, our mission statement, our employee handbook policies, and our setup in the lobby all had to be deconstructed and realigned. By the way, this process will never end. It is an ongoing fight to the death of always keeping the main purpose at the center of the mark.

Don't Be Those Kings

If you examine the books of 1 and 2 Kings, you'll notice a theme. Some kings did what pleased the Lord, others did what displeased the Lord. A few of the good kings tore down the high places, but most did not. These high places were shrines of pagan worship, idols aimed at giving glory to something other than the one true God.

This theme plays out in the twenty-first century as well. Though our idolatry looks different, the heart behind it is the same. Idolatry might not be Asherah poles, shrines built on the tops of mountains, or otherwise, but it might be programming, structures, facilities we've built, or ministries we've partnered with for dozens of years. We have a knack for taking something that has impact and lifting that something above the God it is intended to glorify. Jesus even called it out in the religious leaders of his day: "You search the Sriptures because you think they give you eternal life. But the Scriptures point to me! Yet you refuse to come to me to receive this life" (John 5:39–40, NLT).

As leaders, we often face this challenge as we align our organizations to new visions, new teams, and new plans. Let me paraphrase Jesus' words in another way: "You say that Sunday school, hymns, and your favorite missions organization are the key to the growth of Jesus' church. But the church isn't taking ground! Jesus didn't use Sunday school, hymns, or your favorite missions organizations; those are all man-made. He made disciples in relationship! Yet you refuse to accept Jesus' method and tear down the programmatic idols of your day."

Tearing something down sounds violent. It has a connotation of destruction involving sledgehammers, pickaxes, and arduous work. And to an extent there's truth to that. But how do we value relationship and tear down something that is deeply seeded in someone's heart? How can we lead people through the tearing down and rooting out of something we perceive to be idolatry yet they perceive to be life-giving? It's a tall order for any leader. I'm not suggesting everything that "has been" is wrong or evil. Of course not! I am suggesting, however, that we cannot simply bolt on Jesus' methods to what we're doing and still expect Jesus' results.

There is a fair bit of tearing down that must happen as we align our organizations and churches to what Jesus calls us to be. In the Old Testament, those kings who did not do the hard work of tearing down the high places passed on only to allow the trees of idolatry to sprout up again and again in the kingdoms they led.

Leaders, don't be those kings! Idolatry is still in Jesus' church, and it is more than food, money, sex, etc. Idolatry is much more subtle than that. For some it is church "as it's always been done." That high place must be torn down for our churches to experience the new life waiting for us as we fully obey Jesus and align to his methods for making disciples.

8

TEARING DOWN THE HIGH PLACES: TEARING THEM DOWN

Our congregation had three worship services for years, but our attendance was declining. Senior adults primarily attended our early 8:00 a.m. service. They were faithful, loved their routine, and had been promised the music in that hour would look different than our other two gatherings. That promise was made with no intention to bless or care for them but to pacify and keep happy those who gave consistently to "the mission."

Honestly, I'm not sure of the real intention of keeping the promise in the first place. For years after I arrived on the scene, I was asked, "When are we going to do what was promised to us for this worship gathering?" It had moved from promise made to promise broken and had really hurt some of our most faithful. If we're honest, it was also a high place in our church—an idol. People believed, and some still do, that the style of worship on a Sunday morning is what makes disciples and grows the church. It was time to make a tough decision and ensure that our congregation was aligned to the mission.

I realize this would not be in anyone's playbook for a new senior pastor right out of the gate. My wife was very quick to remind me of that! But it was one example of many that would require patient, careful, intentional leadership to remove ministries and programs that were no longer fruitful, and to give people opportunity to join us in what was.

The leaders called a special meeting to invite those attendees into the vision for the greater mission. I shared that the other services were experiencing baptisms; they didn't know. The other services were experiencing new families; they didn't know. I told them I needed them to join with the rest of the bride that was teeming with life. I needed them to care for and welcome those new families. I desired that they be part of our baptism celebrations and know that new life was happening.

The tone in the room was initially hostile and resistant, but I've learned to listen for the voices of hope in these situations, and they were there. One longtime member seemed to share the conviction, making a plea with her fellow eight o'clockers to merge themselves with the heartbeat of the church. She asked them to lay aside whatever preference it was that kept them isolated from the life that pulsed in the other services. We didn't do away with the 8:00 a.m. service that evening. In fact, more than four months passed before we integrated our 8:00 a.m. service into our other gathering times. Even more amazing, all of those affected by this transition stayed at our church. In our commitment we remained patient and loving, and eventually the church made the shift.

MOPS, Recovery Ministry, and Sunday School

When The MET launched small groups, we had multiple ministries that existed with the intention of creating relationships. However, they lacked the intentional approach we found in small groups. The tension we faced was to abruptly stop these ministries, damaging relationships with those who valued these ministries, or to slowly back away from resourcing these ministries until they eventually "died."

One such ministry was MOPS (Mothers of Preschoolers), a nationwide ministry that provided guidance, support, and multiple resources for churches who wanted to care for this group of moms. We had hosted this ministry for twenty years at The MET, so it had gained a following of leadership and popularity from our community. We had three key observations when we examined the track record of MOPS. First, the audience was exclusive in the sense that it didn't have a place for all mothers, only mothers of this age group who were typically stay-at-home moms. Second, the language used could be confused with what we offered in our small groups. Finally, we recognized the program itself competed with what we were trying to build in groups.

Leadership from the church had individual meetings with MOPS leaders, sharing the vision and informing them that we would not be resourcing them financially in the next budget year. This was hard to digest for some, yet it was the organizational alignment needed to force a ministry to die so the church could have growth in the priority focus. As you know from your own personal time investment and personal budget, you cannot do all the good things that you sometimes seek to do. Intentional, and often painful, decisions go into prioritizing the best thing for maximum fruitfulness.

Eventually, the church leadership was able to rebuild a ministry to mothers that encompassed a greater funnel of women— working moms, stay-at-home moms, and mothers of all ages. It also was able to keep discipleship as the primary goal and served as a funnel to women's small groups. But MOPS as it was previously established, numerically large as it was, needed to be set aside as a good thing to make room for the most important thing.

As the process of turning the church toward relational discipleship continued, it didn't take long to realize the critical importance of biblical counseling resources as well as recovery ministry. The importance of hope-filled, restorative ministries pointing people to their personal healing is essential. These ministries normalize brokenness and direct people to the restorative, transforming power of Jesus. Recovery ministry had previously existed at The MET, but at the time that relational discipleship was seeding, the church's recovery ministry was disconnected from the main mission and siloed unto itself.

Recovery ministry that wasn't purged of codependency and connected to a greater purpose than existing for recovery ministry alone wouldn't get us where we were going. Upon careful examination and several critical conversations, recovery ministry as it had been at The MET needed to be released. It had to be rebuilt and fueled with the focus of essential connection to the bride and the greater mission of relational discipleship. It took some time, but eventually our Regeneration ministry was launched with the mission of making disciples at the forefront.

And then there was the granddaddy of all. If there was one shift that took the longest, logged the most hours in meetings and discussions, consumed the most coffees and lunches, and faced the most resistance, it was Sunday school. This ministry was the most difficult in which to birth the new vision. It was fraught with tears, emotion, and pain and was tied to relationship for so many.

Sunday school had been the vehicle of biblical education for churches in my denomination for over a century. And besides biblical education, some classes had cultivated many elements of a fruitful church—care, development of spiritual disciplines, and fellowship. But the Sunday school model consistently lacked a reproducible process. For the vast majority, Sunday school classes had become places of great stability and connection for our longtime members. They had become a place of comfort, in both a positive and negative way, and the tension of mission, outreach, and discipleship had been lost. I didn't see the lost being grafted in and grown up. I didn't see faith being replicated in others. I didn't see members characterized by an outward focus. All I saw was the transfer of biblical knowledge but no evidence of fruitful discipleship for the most part.

Because these classes had been havens for many members for many years, the engagement of alignment in this domain was intentionally slower than any of the others. It took over seven years. As I mentioned earlier, the meetings were countless. First, we invited the teachers into the bigger vision, and then over time, met with all classes, individual classes, and individual couples. The heat and anger affiliated with this piece of alignment burned and scalded the most, both me and those opposed, I suppose. Some grieved over what they had experienced and longed to continue. However, they acknowledged the idea of having only gifted, called teachers who taught the Bible with intentional topics and edified the entirety of the body, as opposed to every class doing its own thing.

But no matter how much I held up the vision of connecting people in a relational environment for the purpose of discipleship, the hot tears flowed and anger flared. The perception was that I had thrown a stick of dynamite into their longtime circle of friendships, demanding that they go their separate ways. I don't know if it was obstinance on their part, ineffective communication on my part, or both, but my heart is still sore from some of these conversations.

Some members in faith pivoted to the mission and started small groups with a nucleus of Sunday school class members. Others huddled up under the banner of their previous class in various places, including meeting at other churches. I share this with some embarrassment and sadness, but also transparency of the challenge at hand. Getting bogged down in this standoff for so long sometimes made me want to call it quits. But the fruitfulness I saw in those who pivoted, and the light and life I saw in the vibrancy of those engaging mission, made it worth it. Those who had fallen asleep in habit and routine were now awake to the mission of being disciples who make disciples both in the body and in God's kingdom.

Multisite and Church Planting

When it comes to multisite or church planting, I don't believe it has to be one or the other. In our situation, however, we had to decide which aligned more to our mission. We were a multisite church with just two campuses. But as relational discipleship took form in our hearts and in our practices, we knew that we would have to practice corporately what we celebrated privately—the branching of a church into her own self-sustaining, disciple-making church.

The decision was unpopular on several fronts. Many pastor friends told me I'd made a bad business decision. On top of that, several from our second campus were not excited about being "left out on their own." They had moved out there from the main campus as a personal mission, and now we appeared to be abandoning them! But we knew the decision to model corporately what we elevated in our small-group culture was the right direction to take. It would be a testimony to the strength and reproducibility of Jesus' methods for making disciples.

We didn't include several staff in our new vision, which caused some tensions that were only resolved with their departure from the team—a tough, grueling, and relationally exhausting experience. Long-standing relationships changed in an instant, but our commitment was unwavering. We had previously elected two elders from the sister campus in Cypress to serve alongside the elders from the main campus. This would ensure the DNA of relationship would be at the forefront of both organizations as we moved ahead.

Our final step before branching the campus was hiring another senior pastor. He would serve alongside us for a year, and then as the transition was made, he would step into senior leadership of that campus. I must admit, I could have done this differently. Bob was a twenty-year veteran of ministry and leadership. He bled relational discipleship and had even served on the board of the Relational Discipleship Network. I regret not making his and my relationship more of a priority upon his arrival, especially during those formative months. Our relationship would have spoken and modeled exactly what we preach so intentionally, but I didn't prioritize it. My absence also communicated a message of abandonment to the staff on that campus. They had stayed. They had weathered the storm, and we were about to see it all come to fruition, but I had moved on too quickly. I have since apologized, and we have mended relationships, but I missed an opportunity for me and that staff, and I regret that.

With that said, the decision to branch this church proved to be one of the most aligning, catalyzing experiences for both campuses, now fully autonomous churches. It required sacrifice from both churches. It took commitment to relationship, above everything else, from both churches, and it allowed both places to function in their unique communities, ministering to the unique needs around them, with full autonomy. It allowed Jesus' message and methods to be the foundational cornerstone of both places, though their organizational and community footprints look so different. God is so redemptive, and his church is so beautiful.

Missions

I could cry as I sit and type these words. The story of God's birthing the new framework for missions at The MET with a lens of relational discipleship is one of my favorite stories of this process. When I became the senior pastor at our church, The MET comprised two campuses at the time: the fifty-year-old campus and a new campus in a fast-growing area of our city. The MET's heritage in missions was well-known in the area. We were a very missional church, at least by my standards at the time. We built orphanages overseas, sponsored camps in the Philippines that saw thousands come to Christ, built churches in Mexico, and funded an evangelical radio station in Africa that took the gospel into villages and schools, not to mention the more than forty-five organizations to whom we wrote regular checks from our missions budget.

During the previous pastor's departure, he took with him several of these initiatives, and we chose to walk away from some of the others. Why? Because I didn't feel that they were truly aligned with where the Lord was directing our church. I knew we had to walk away from some of these long-standing relationships and forge a new path, where our mission was on display in absolutely everything we did.

Despite being affiliated with many mission projects and generously giving to those, we still seemed to be extremely inward facing. We looked like so many churches out there. We were relational with the world, but we were not necessarily in relationship with the world. We were helping other nonprofits and NGOs worldwide accomplish their vision and mission, but what about the mission God had given us as his local church? We had seen God do some incredible work in our midst as it pertained to relational discipleship, and I wanted to see this take root all over the world, but how? Writing a check to a larger entity would not train my people to be more missional. If anything, it would keep it from them, or relegate it to their ability to give rather than their heart to go. Both are extremely important, but to grow spiritually, we needed the latter more than the former.

I began to ask God, "Would you please confirm our mission? Would you birth a mission from here, from within this church, one that we can rally behind together?" We were in the holiday season, and I was looking for some God stories. These were stories that really solidified our vision for making disciples in meaningful relationship. I told our staff to keep their eyes open as they talked to men and women in the church lobbies or at lunch during the weeks that progressed. I wanted us to collect as many as we could.

After sharing this with my staff, one of our pastors, Derrick, reached out to me. "Matt, you need to talk to Richard! The guy is on fire for Jesus, and relational discipleship has changed his life. He's having serious conversations with me about what you asked for, and you need to reach out to him!"

Shortly thereafter, my family was en route to Oklahoma for Thanksgiving when Richard and I connected via phone. Richard had been at our church for a few short years, here on assignment from Germany with his company. He and his family were actively pursuing the Lord, getting more and more involved, and he and I had spent some intentional time together weekly in a discipleship relationship. To say he was on the fast track would be an understatement.

Richard was full of life. He had a thick German accent and the heart of a lion but was gentle in speech and spirit. His hair was red as fire, and his smile was warm enough to light it. So when he called as we were driving, I thought the conversation would be nothing more than a relational connection with a guy I had been doing life with for a season. I picked up the phone, and we talked for more than forty-five minutes.

With passion and emotion in his voice, he told me he was hearing a whisper from the Holy Spirit. God wanted him to take this intentional, relational discipleship model back to his home in Germany. I looked over at my wife, both eyebrows raised to the roof of my vehicle, and tears began rolling down my cheek. God had confirmed my request for a mission opportunity through this brother in Christ, and I was watching God work right in front of my eyes. I was so excited, humbled, fired up, and in awe all at the same time. I told Richard what I had prayed, and how God had answered my prayer.

That was four years ago. Since then, and despite a global pandemic, we have had intentional relationships with five churches near Cologne, Germany, and the surrounding area. Several German leaders have flown to Houston to participate in a national DiscipleShift 1 conference at our church. We had the privilege of hosting a German family in our residency program for a year. And now, one of our staff members and his family currently live in Germany on mission. They cultivate and continually model relational discipleship.

I go back with teams each year when I am able and will do so for the duration of my ministry. Why? For the sake of meaningful relationships. I have built lifelong friendships with Richard (now back home in Germany and living missionally while working his secular job); Andre (pastor in Siegburg); Harry, Daniel, and Bernhard (pastors in Gummersbach); Markus, Anna, Felix, and Nora (elder family in Siegburg); and countless others in their churches. Most exciting to me—a church has been planted in Lohmar through the obedience of Richard and local leaders to live out the mission of making disciples in meaningful relationship. God is moving. He is equipping, he is exhorting, he is encouraging, he is empowering, he is opening doors, he is going before us, and he is building bridges across the Atlantic—for his glory. It is and always will be only for his glory.

Had I not followed the prompting of the Holy Spirit to step away from our previous missions strategy for the sake of alignment and agreed to meet with Richard regularly, and had Richard not followed the prompting of the Spirit in the same way, think about what we would have missed. I feel like it's just getting started.

Alignment costs us every time, but it's an investment worth making in every area of the ministries we lead. In fact, I would argue that we cannot afford to fail in this endeavor. Align every ministry to your mission. Pay the price, and then reap the reward.

9

THE MISSION HASN'T CHANGED

When Jesus called his first disciples, there was never any doubt of the mission, and this was long before he died, was buried, rose from the dead, and ascended. Matthew 4:19 says, "Come, follow me, and I will make you fishers of men." My brothers and sisters at Real Life Ministries in Post Falls, Idaho, taught me that the definition of a disciple of Christ was in his initial invitation. As a staff, we used the following three tenets of Jesus' ministry as the funnel through which we shifted our church from being a business model to being in the business of making disciples.

Come, Follow Me

A disciple of Jesus is one who knows and is following Christ. Knowing Christ is about that intimate connection one has with the person of Jesus. The moment of conversion was an introduction, but that was just the beginning. It is not just a lifetime of learning about him but also an intentional pursuit of intimacy with Christ, giving him access to me—all of me. As he reveals himself to me, and I learn more about his ways and character, I align my life to submitting to his ways. My habits, my relationships, and my framework for life look different. They have substance and fruitfulness that they didn't have previously. I am continually in the process of following in his steps. Great leaders are always great followers first.

And I Will Make You

A disciple of Jesus is one who is constantly being changed by Christ. When Jesus said, "I will make," he referenced the process of knowing and following Christ. As those new relationships, habits, and disciplines form, they also form us. A commitment to follow Jesus is also a commitment to being changed by Jesus. Some personal practices, preferences, and relationships now must look different. I must humbly submit my life and leadership to the changes that Jesus makes. Sounds simple, right? But we know the continually dying to self and embracing sanctification is anything but easy.

We experienced this challenge within our organization many times. Jesus guided us, and our elders and staff sought to submit to his leading fully. It often brought us to crossroads, and some didn't want to step into the new reality for fear of what it would cost. It's really what the stories of this book are all about. As Jesus transforms us, and our church submits to the leadership of the Good Shepherd, we recognize the need to align fully. When we fail to align to our leader, we fail to follow. When we fail to follow, we do not experience the transformation he desires for us and the organizations we lead.

The voice of Jesus is often polarizing. The changes that Jesus requests are not always small tweaks. Sometimes they are radical shifts. But the call to follow is the call to being changed. A disciple-making church must make those changes with resolve. Grit will wane and strength will run out, but the resolve to obey and commit to the changes must be present to shift a culture.

Fishers of Men

A disciple of Jesus is one who is committed to the mission of Christ. The mission of Christ, making disciples of all nations, came clearly from the lips of Jesus in Matthew 28:19–20. Making disciples is the clear purpose of Jesus' church. Mission drift, however, is a dreaded predicament too many of us have seen and experienced. I have seen it in my life from my marriage and parenting to the way I love my neighbor and support my extended family. So many things vie for our attention, things that pull us away from living and leading missionally. Living and leading missionally is a grind. It takes a level of forethought, a level of intentionality and intensity that few of us master fully. It is so much easier to throw an event and share the gospel than to invite ministries to connect people to meaningful relationship and walk alongside someone.

For example, we know how to throw a community-wide event, rent out the biggest bounce houses we can find, order a petting zoo for the littles, and invite the fire department to make a makeshift splash pad. Then we just attach a gospel message to it. It's just easier. We get railroaded by the intentionality of Jesus' missional request in Matthew 28 when we are told to make disciples of all nations—instead of converts. But we can't be about the message of Jesus without the methods of Jesus. And as pure-hearted as our intentions may be, we are in most cases out to sea.

I can hear the internal frustration build as you read this. I am in no way attacking the character of ministers in any denomination, nor the calling and heartbeat for the lost that God gives to those serving in such capacities. I am simply pointing out that what we've done programmatically throughout the years, even with pure motives, has not necessarily produced the fruit Jesus intended. As disciple makers, we must reset priorities, schedules, times with God, habits, and thought processes. Disciple makers must submit to that process and learn to embrace the change personally, as well as in all areas in which they lead. When we do, the fruit, the joy, and the passion increase exponentially.

Jesus knew what he was doing. We can no longer hide behind ignorance. Jesus was clear when he called the Twelve, sent out the Seventy-Two, and sent the Holy Spirit to fall on the church in Acts. His message was compelling, and his methods were proven.

Relational discipleship happens in the raw moments of life. It's not relegated to an hour on Sunday, a Bible study on Wednesday mornings, or an appointment in the pastor's office or with a professional counselor. Relationship and discipleship pair best in the proximity of people doing everyday life together. For me, it can be on a softball field as my daughter's coach, in a golf cart with a friend, or on vacation with my wife. It's doing life together even in the parts that aren't perfect or polished. No matter what, we keep loving each other, fighting for each other, and providing safety for each other.

Years ago, discipleship looked like a pastor or expert teacher rattling off facts while students dutifully took notes. If that method had been entirely effective, we wouldn't have the statistics we have today of unchurched people and the generations that no longer attend church. Jesus' first disciples were not deep philosophers, were not all experts in the law, were not great orators, and were not the most knowledgeable or noble of persons. They were common. I find great acceptance and freedom in who Jesus chose to follow him. Knowledge has its place, but that knowledge must both travel to and dwell within the heart. Knowledge must manifest itself in how we treat others by accepting, forgiving, and literally loving our neighbor as ourselves.

Consider Judas. He spent three years with Jesus. He watched Jesus, spent time with him, and experienced unconditional love in a way only eleven others did. He had the opportunity to emulate Jesus' example, yet he didn't. His heart's desire was bent toward money and power rather than suffering and sacrifice. It's what compelled him to sell Jesus out to the Pharisees, and his heart's focus cost him a life full of love, purpose, and mission.

Jesus wants us—all of us. He wants a heart yielded to him, but he always respects our decision to choose him or not. This is why, before the crowd dragged Jesus away, he told Judas, "Do what you came here to do." Jesus knew Judas's heart. He knew

Judas cared more about power and wealth than he did about a Savior who had invested in him.

Earlier in the book I shared about my relationship with Jason. I chose to invest in him because his heart desired to know more about Jesus. Jason proved himself to be faithful, available, and teachable. Since our time together, Jason has started several small groups and discipled dozens of men in our church. He took the example we set for him, and he chose to follow in our footsteps. A critical principle of discipleship is that each person gets to decide what they are going to invest in the process. Each person has the freedom to choose, just like God gives us freedom to choose him.

The people with whom we engage in meaningful relationship may choose to follow our direction, or they may choose to go their own way. They can say all the right things and spend years with us, but when it comes to following Jesus on their own, it depends on where their desire lies. They may follow his direction or go their own way. It's up to them.

In my relationship with Jason, I did my part. I was available for him, answered his questions to the best of my ability with God's Word, and invested in our time together. Jason did his part; he grew because he wanted to grow. He wanted to grow because he had people in his corner who rooted for him, encouraged him, and challenged him. And God always does his part. God revealed new truths, habits, and direction to both Jason and me as it pertained to next steps for each of us. There was true, biblical community with God and each other, and it was meaningful.

10

MISSION OVER METRICS

The MET was born more than fifty years ago in someone's living room with six couples who shared a sincere desire to see a life-giving, thriving church in Northwest Houston. All these years later, we are still here, standing on the shoulders of those with enough vision, grit, and determination to see this church grow, pivot, shift, and continue to take ground for God's kingdom year after year. Over time, we had drifted from our ultimate calling. Our business meetings became more about agendas and business items rather than deeply caring about each other. As a staff, we brainstormed and realized this was not the church we wanted to lead. If we wanted to realign ourselves with Jesus' mission, we would have to embrace three new shifts: relationships over results, check-ins over paychecks, and mission over metrics.

Recently, we had an exercise with some of our church staff. I asked, "What is the difference between qualitative and quantitative metrics?" Staff members gave answers such as attendance, the amount of money given for the missions offering, and kids' salvation numbers. Our children's pastor, Hannah, then answered the question "What's an example of a qualitative metric?" with this answer: "When a child lets go of their parent's hand and runs to their teacher."

Her response deeply touched me. But what does that mean? Together, we came up with four qualitative results based on that response:

- Trust between child and teacher (and parent and teacher)
- An innate sense of safety and love in that volunteer's presence
- An active, positive relationship between each party
- Building rapport between volunteer and child

The best results from discipleship can't always be tallied on a piece of paper or added to the church attendance matrix. The church of the New Testament is not where people go; it's who the people are. The healthier the church, then the healthier the community becomes, the welfare of the community is blessed, and the glory of the Lord shines brightly.

In discipleship, three people are involved: myself, the person I'm discipling, and God. Each person has their part to play. However, it gets more difficult because there is a bit of an overlap. When we try to be the transforming agent in someone's life, failure usually follows. Our part is to disciple and cultivate; God's part is to transform the heart.

Think about Judas. Even though he spent time with Jesus and did everything the other disciples did, he still sold out. Relational discipleship involves an investment. It involves an investment of time, money, and resources for the sake of the gospel. To adopt a relational discipleship model, here are some of the elements you will need to invest in:

- Faithfulness
- Empathy
- Follow-through
- Humility

We must do our part in relational discipleship; God is always faithful to do his part. But the person being discipled has a part as well. They must humble themselves and submit to those principles and commit to the process. The problem becomes when we want it more than the person being discipled. We can't want something for someone else. They must want it; we can't want it for them.

When it comes to discipleship through relationship, we will find those who quickly adopt our counsel, our habits, new truths we share, etc. But we will also find those unwilling to do their part. That's when it gets painful. It happened to Jesus with Judas, and even Peter had moments of denial. The struggle is real. As leaders we can do our part to cast a compelling vision and pray and ask the Lord to convince those we shepherd to get on board. But ultimately, they all must do their part to adapt and adopt the new reality.

As leaders, it is easy to blame ourselves and turn inward, allowing our internal dialogue to go like this: *Maybe I did it wrong because I didn't get the result.* The reality is we can do it all right and not get the results we desire. The only thing we can do is to yield our lives to Christ's will, love others well, invest our lives in them, and equip them to make disciples.

Leaders tend to see church as a process. We ask questions at leadership meetings such as, "What's the right kind of structure? What's the right kind of small group? What's the best curriculum to implement into our Sunday school?"

But there's a better model. Ask questions such as "Who has God put on the radar of my heart this morning?" or "Have I called and checked in on the people of my church this week at all?" It's a bit messier but so much more rewarding. It also shifts our metric mindset as leaders.

If we're honest, we like the metrics. We don't like the messiness and unpredictability of people. We like the safety of a measurable outcome. We like knowing that the formula, when applied in the same way, produces the same result every time. Until, of course, it doesn't.

Daniel Im, author of *No Silver Bullets*, says:

> The most common way that churches measure discipleship is through the use of output goals. Metrics like participation in a small group or Sunday School class, how often one attends weekend worship, how much one gives, whether one is serving, and if one is baptized are

some of the most common output goals that churches measure. This is obviously much better than having no metrics at all, since you can measure these goals week over week, month over month, or year over year to see progress. Unfortunately, output goals in and of themselves don't move people towards Christ! *Output goals are the results of input goals.* If all you do is focus on output goals and let everyone choose their own input goals, you won't be able to reproduce any success that you might encounter. Let me say this a different way—a metric is not a good goal. It doesn't produce the fruit we're called to produce as followers of Jesus. It simply shows us a dashboard as to whether we're hitting the mark.[5]

A better model is just that—a model. But it's not a better mental model, not a process or organizational structure that points people to the right mission. Disciples are the ultimate model. That's why it always begins with people. We must model what we expect others to be and do. That's how Jesus did it. Organizational structures and boards, leadership teams and team leaders all must model that the process takes a back seat to the people. This was the first big shift for our church.

Don't begin with the agenda of man. It will distract you from the agenda of God too often. Begin with what God is doing in people's lives and allow the fruit of that work to guide you to the vision for your organization. But you must know others and be known by others for that to take root in your organization.

Here are a few critical questions that might help you get started in your next meeting:

- "What has God done in your life in the past week?" (We call these "God stories.")
- "What is God teaching you about himself right now?"
- "What are you reading in the Word right now?"
- "Whom do you identify with in Scripture right now, and why?"

Ditch the metrics, the assessments, and the measuring tools. Make people the priority. Honor the process of knowing others intimately and being known by others intimately. Because the work that honors God the most cannot be measured on a piece of paper; instead, it's measured in the disciples who walk out of the door of your church.

The Shift to "Sunday Is Second"

Church = Sunday Morning—or at least that is what I was raised to believe. I grew up thinking church was about wearing my "Sunday best," attending a Bible study, and going to church. My attendance over these few hours put God and me on good terms for the rest of the week, and I was a "good Christian." Over time we relaxed the dress code, made Bible studies look cooler, and transformed worship into something between a concert and a convention. But these updates have not changed the simple truth that most who attend feel today that *Church = Sunday Morning.*

As we began our path toward a relational discipleship culture, we quickly realized this mantra's downfall. Sunday morning was gaining us attendees but not making disciples. Our staff was putting in hundreds of hours per week and thousands of dollars of our resources to produce three hours' worth of programming that made little difference in how someone lived. We needed to make a significant shift.

Rick Theriot, pastor of assimilation at The MET, said:

> We changed our mentality to "Sunday is second." This means that what happens on Sunday is second to the discipleship and life change that occurs throughout the week. This new mantra has adjusted how we spend our time, how we hire, how we budget, and what we celebrate. We celebrate stories of life change, not attendance numbers. We have reduced our spending on worship and tech and spend more on groups, pastors, and discipleship. Sunday is important because it is still the front door of our church, but it is not our primary avenue of discipleship. Sunday is second because discipleship at any time and any place is first.

This shift has come with battle scars, and we have lost vibrant, life-giving members of this amazing church to other congregations around our city. With that said, there is no way we'd go back to what was. Our alignment in this key area has produced a harvest. It has elevated our ability to shepherd our people with intentionality and has moved our people to a more connected spiritual life. There are still those who slip in and out quietly, and whose only connection to our church is through our weekend gatherings. But we work hard to connect everyone we can, not simply to a Sunday gathering, but to a life-transforming, meaningful relationship with God and each other.

It's hard to be changed. It costs. It hurts. It even offends at times. But it's necessary. Following Jesus demands it.

11

WHO WE ARE

I explained earlier who we were as an organization prior to the shift. Who we are now looks entirely different. The shift has permeated every area of office and ministry at The MET Church. From eldership to pew, the transformation is tangible. God has reworked the heartbeat of our leadership, our staff, and in turn, our congregation. We are a completely different church than we were just eight short years ago, and it's all to the glory of God. As we've aligned every element to the mission and methods of Jesus, the fruit that has been born is unmistakable.

Elders

The MET has been around for more than fifty years, but we have only had elders for the past eight years. Elders are not common within our denomination, and to be honest, I'm not sure why. Our denomination largely moved to a more congregational model of leadership, and it had been that way at The MET for most of her existence. However, when The MET joined the Relational Discipleship Network in 2013, it did so with the understanding that we would move to a biblical model of elder leadership. In 2014, The MET called her first eldership, and it was one of the single greatest leadership moves in our church's history. Today, these men currently lead and display unity that is rarely seen in a congregational model. They love and support our staff while keeping them accountable. They model the relational connection with God and each other that we expect from our staff and our congregation.

Our bylaws state that elders serve three-year terms. They can serve as many as two terms back-to-back, but after this they must take a one-year break. This is for their own personal growth, and if it's been a difficult term, a time of rest as well. During the one-year break, I often look for leaders to replace the current elders once their term is over. They are what I call "DNA carriers."

A DNA carrier builds the church's culture in how they live. The culture of a congregation is its lifeblood and must be built and protected. It is made up of what the church creates, what it celebrates, and what it tolerates. Our elders model what it means to live in close proximity with each other. They pursue the Lord together. Their meetings are geared to build relationships with God and each other. They stop by the office on occasion and check in on our staff throughout the week. They even lead portions of our staff meetings at times, encouraging and equipping us to live out the mission to which we are called.

I remember a particular church member who was not thrilled with something I said from the stage one weekend. He sent me a long email telling me of his disapproval. When I shared it with the elders, the response was almost immediate: "This is not an email-worthy conversation. Which one of us would you like to take with you as you engage this guy in relationship and fight for what matters? It's who we are, Matt, and it begins with us."

What's more, elders are not all literally "elder," meaning not all elders are senior adults. We do have elders in their eighties, but we also have elders in their forties and fifties. And our elders are not simply our clerical staff members; rather, they are the men God has elevated to our attention along the way from all walks of life. Alexander Strauch said it well: "The distinguishing mark of Christianity was not found in a clerical hierarchy, but in the fact that God's Spirit came to dwell within ordinary, common people and that through them the Spirit manifested Jesus' life to the believing community and the world."[6]

As life happens, we've lost some elders along the way. One moved away to Waco and got a new job. Another resigned for personal reasons. When this happens, our eldership keeps close watch for leaders to fill those vacancies with someone who is "eldering" in the way they live. I use "eldering" as a verb because of what I see in the person. I see the characteristics of 1 Timothy 3:2–7 on display in how they lead their families. These men are sober-minded, self-controlled, respectable, and hospitable. They live "above reproach," meaning they are worthy of respect, with no outstanding relational debts to others in how they live. They are available to teach and instruct at a moment's notice, whether it be deep theology or simply how to have a more loving union with the person of Christ. They reject vices, and they are not drunkards, not quarrelsome, and not lovers of money.

In addition to these shining characteristics, I also see how they follow the leadership of our church. I am in awe of how all our current elders are disciple makers in all aspects of their lives. Transformed lives follow them around—it's as if everywhere they go, the mission of making disciples is on display.

Elders look like Jesus in the way they lead. In other words, there is a consistent relational connection to the congregation they lead. They shepherd people carefully and intentionally. They are willing to face critique, and they boldly stand up for the body of Christ. In times of controversy, their intention is unifying the body, not simply winning a church-wide vote. An elder truly understands Jesus' prayer from John 17:

> My prayer is not for them alone. I pray also for those who will believe in me through their message, that all of them may be one, Father, just as you are in me, and I am in you. May they also be in us so that the world may believe that you have sent me. I have given them the glory that you gave me, that they may be one as we are one—I in them and you in me—so that they may be brought to complete unity. Then the world will know that you sent me and have loved them even as you have loved me. (John 17:20–23)

Elders are also committed to a missional mindset. An elder understands the mission of Jesus. They don't simply seek to keep as many people in the seats as possible. Instead, they have a sending mindset. As they invest in others, they do so with intentions to see that person reproduce other disciple makers as well. If a disciple feels called to ministry or to use their spiritual gifts in a capacity outside our congregation, our elders celebrate and even facilitate that transition with joy.

Biblical eldership often flies in the face of the American mindset. Most elders' meetings that I have observed over the years look like boardrooms. While the business of the church is a portion of an elder's responsibility, The MET's mantra is: "This is not a boardroom. It's a stable." As 1 Peter 5:1–3 states, we are here to care for the flock whom God has given us to lead and guide. Eldership is a spiritual task first, not simply a fiduciary responsibility. At least once a year, we have our "back to reality" conversation, grounding our hearts and minds in what it means to shepherd the people under our care. Thus, we live out the mission and a life of servanthood leadership. We allow the staff to run the affairs of the church while we shepherd and care for the flock. This includes spiritual direction for teaching in our weekend services. This includes our master plan and how we align our facilities to the mission God has given us. But it also means participating in the mission personally, growing people up in Christ, and sending them out to do the same.

Richie is a perfect example of what it means to live out leadership as an elder. He and his wife love so many people well. They disciple others in relational small groups and have branched small groups because of their leadership. I've seen the men who come out of Richie's care. They show tremendous leadership potential and hearts for the mission of Jesus. Richie is not just an elder; he's "eldering."

Deacons

For many congregations, deacons play multiple roles. They serve, but they are also the leadership of the church, especially in the congregational model. We had a more staff-led model at the time of our shift, and the deacons were—and remain today— what I like to call first responders. In other words, we ask our deacons to go first. Whether modeling a posture of servanthood, being the first responders during our worship services to those making life-changing decisions, or being the first to champion a new vision, deacons are first responders. This shift is still in process but is making progress. We are developing a new identity and even building a similar culture for our staff within our deacon body. We are crafting language that catalyzes action and rallies the troops. Our deacons are a force of good in our church. They pave the way for those who need to see an example of what following really looks like, and they are getting better at it every day.

Staff

Establishing a spiritual covering in our eldership has been critical for our church. Along with restricting our leadership model and mission statement, we set out to establish key virtues to shape our mentality and define our non-negotiables as an eldership and a staff. As we pursued our mission and vision both in the city of Houston and around the world, we landed on five virtues that should embody the *heart* of our elders and church staff. These virtues are now the standard by which we assess our efforts through the lens of our mission. We use HEART as an acronym to keep it memorable and simple.

H – Humility. Most sins turn us away from God, but pride is a direct attack upon God. It lifts our hearts above him and against him. Pride seeks to dethrone God and enthrone self. Humility is a modesty of one's own importance. When it comes to being the church, humility is how we view ourselves in relationship to God.

Humility is an unmistakable character trait seen throughout the Scriptures. For example, James 4:6 states, "God opposes the proud but gives grace to the humble" (ESV). Where pride offers God's opposition as followers of Jesus, humility removes God's opposition and brings God's grace, blessing, wisdom, honor, answers to prayers, and clear direction. God exalts those who are humble. It is the quintessential character trait of one who knows and follows Christ. Humble people are teachable, don't act out of selfish ambition, and agree with what God says about who they are. They have an appetite to serve others.

E – Effectiveness. Peter Drucker once said, "Efficiency is doing things right; effectiveness is doing the right things."[7] Effectiveness in ministry implies that we have our eyes set on the right target. For us, that is to make disciples of Jesus who can go and make other disciples of Jesus.

With a clear vision, effectiveness then demands that we always give God our absolute best. It asks us to increase our capacity, our work ethic, and our hustle. Effectiveness values excellence, innovation, and creativity at a high level, because we cannot remain effective and continue to do things the same way as the landscape arounds us changes constantly. This also means we constantly evaluate all we do and engage in crucial conversations to make the organization better and push the mission forward in the best possible way.

Effectiveness demands that people view all goals and tasks through the lens of mission, but they also get things done without damaging relationships. It asks that leaders give their best in all they do and put their whole hearts into their work. Finally, effective people understand the value of reinvention. They understand change and its necessity in leadership. This has obviously been a critical value in our pivot to relational discipleship.

A – Awe. God created us to experience awe, not just of anything, but awe of him. Psalm 145:4 says, "One generation will commend your works to another." Paul David Tripp wrote, "God intends every moment of ministry to inspire awe of himself in his people."[8] If everything we do doesn't point people to an awe of God, it is broken. From kids' programming to songs in a worship service, from the exegesis of Scripture to a question and conversation in our living room, we must always do our part to point people to the magnitude, grace, and glory of God.

People who live in awe are worshipers. They never miss an opportunity to magnify Christ. They never forget who God is, and they abide in Christ by spending time in his Word, worshiping, meditating, and praying. They view ministry as a "get to" rather than a "have to." People who live in awe of God preach the gospel to themselves regularly, constantly reminding themselves of the grace that's been lavished on them. They stay anchored in perspective when feelings are hurt or when disappointment comes from the changes around them. Finally, people who live in awe of God listen to his voice above all others in their lives. This is critical for the church of Jesus.

R – Relationship. In Genesis 2:18, we see the first real crisis in Scripture. God looked at man and said, "It is not good for the man to be alone." Here we see that God hardwired humans for relationships—first for a relationship with God, and then for a relationship with each other. Because of this truth, we hold tightly to discipling people in the context of meaningful relationships.

The relationships we have are true gifts from the Father. With this in mind, we do everything we can to protect relationships, fight for relationships, and value relationships at the highest level. If we accomplish a task or reach a goal, but sacrifice people to get there, we have failed. Getting relationships right is imperative.

In John 13:35, Jesus said, "By this everyone will know that you are my disciples, if you love one another." People who value relationships show honor to one another. People who value relationships take others with them when ministering, seizing every opportunity to invest in and equip those they lead. They are quick to forgive and consistently share the truth in love. They recognize that growing spiritually demands growing in relationship not only with God but with others as well.

T – Truth. Truth is the plumb line. God's Word is truth. Warren W. Wiersbe wrote, "It has been well said that truth without love is brutality and love without truth is hypocrisy."[9] We value truth at the highest level. We value truth in our circumstances as well as in our relationships. We only share what is true with others, and we do so in love. We are authentic with ourselves and others, and we represent that accurately. We are honest about our struggles, our shortcomings, our mistakes, and our evaluations of the ministries God has given us to steward. Whether speaking on a stage or leading a team meeting, we seek truth in everything we do.

People who live out the virtue of truth use God's Word as the foundation for everything they do. They are honest in their assessment of themselves and others. They are willing to engage in transparent, vulnerable conversations, even willing to confront the facts regardless of the outcome. And when truth comes under attack, they are willing and ready to defend it.

Small Groups

We knew we needed to create an environment where people could not only do life together and build lifelong relationships but also replicate disciple-making leaders. We slowly began to live out our new missional calling in small groups. Due to our diligence in training leaders, it wasn't long before we saw growth. Two small groups quickly became twelve, twelve became thirty-six, and in just a few short years, thirty-six multiplied to seventy-five!

We believe small groups are the best way to make disciples and pinpoint potential leaders, so we stayed the course. That decision proved vital to our alignment to God's mission, and we haven't looked back since.

12

STAY, SHIFT, LOVE, AND LIFT

Dr. Joe Ligon, former pastor of First Baptist Church in Marlow, Oklahoma, once told me, "If something catastrophic were to happen to this church, I pray that the city around us would mourn the loss." As stated earlier, The MET began in the living room of a godly couple who knew a population of people was moving outward toward the suburbs. They believed the booming surge would need a thriving church . . . and for most churches, that's why and where they plant. They go where the money is, and why not? God is everywhere, right?

But as a community shifts, as its economic status changes and changes again, a church that lives within a community must also embrace the change. If she does not embrace what the community *is*, she fails to meet her first priority: to bring Jesus to the people she lives among and is called to serve. Many churches treat Sunday attendance as the great success metric. They budget, plan for, and celebrate attendance more than almost anything else. This must shift. It's not simply about coming to church but also being the church. The community does not exist for the church; the church exists for the community.

Near the end of 2021, I cast a new vision for The MET Church regarding our role in serving the community. I came up with the strategy to "stay, shift, love, and lift." It was a cry for our people to truly engage the city with a new sense of intentionality. As the church goes, the community goes. I truly believe this.

Stay

Don't plant elsewhere, don't move to where the affluent are moving, and don't see your area's changing as a threat. Jesus' message and methods are transcendent and are exactly what the people of your community need. Of course, it's easier to grow numerically when we go to where population increase is happening. It strokes our egos and truly points to the value system in America: what's new trumps what's old . . . we want the latest, greatest, biggest, and best. All while the have-nots of our cities are not aided in *their* pursuit of a better life. They're more of a mission trip rather than a mission. The community around the church that embraces relational discipleship should feel the shift.

Shift

As our community shifts, we must outpace the shift. We must beat the community to the punch. We must be there waiting with the gospel, with the hope of meaningful relationship with

God and each other in hand, ready to give to all who will willingly submit to Jesus and all he has for them.

What used to work in affluent areas will not necessarily work anymore—will we shift? As we grow more ethnically diverse, our worship styles and services might need an overhaul—will we shift? Sunday school with people who are just like us might not be the most effective way for getting people to engage God's Word and its life-transforming power—will we shift? As our schools grow in numbers with families whose budgets are doing just the opposite, our ministry offerings might need to look very different—will we shift?

We must.

Love

Throughout the New Testament, Jesus and his disciples made it extremely clear that love of God and love of each other is the most magnetic, winsome characteristic of a follower of Jesus. It speaks to the way we treat those who are first-time guests. It informs the way we worship the Lord together. It is the glue that holds us together and teaches us to fight for real, meaningful relationship during trials. Love never fails.

Conversely, the lack of true love is the demise of the church. If our city is going to receive any message or ministry from us, she must believe that we are for her and that we love her with all our hearts. Loving a community is about the selfless way that we give of ourselves so she can be better. It is the thoughtful way that we choose to engage local schools and businesses. It is the creativity and pursuit of her heart through radical generosity. And it never fails. One more time: love never fails.

Lift

Jeremiah 29 speaks of a time when God's people were in captivity. Amid their challenges, God issued a decree for the people to seek to lift the city. He commanded them to build houses, take wives and husbands, and plant gardens. In other words, they were to love where they lived.

Lifting a city means that what we do is for someone else. We benefit, but the city feels the weight on her shoulders begin to lighten as she is in relationship with Jesus' church. The challenges of this world continue to increase. It is more challenging to live and to lead now than ever before. Yet Jesus said his yoke is easy and his burden is light. As we represent Jesus to this city and as we learn to live in meaningful relationship with them, the weight of their circumstances and challenges should lighten. We exist to lift the city.

Over the course of the last five years, relational discipleship has taken root in our local church. We have experienced some of the most meaningful relationships with our community and community partners that I have ever seen. We said yes when Hurricane Harvey hit our city and were a shelter for more than nine hundred people for two full weeks. We housed a feeding center as well as medical and vet clinics, and we transformed our facility into one of the largest relief shelters in our area during a devastating time for our city. We provide meals during holiday seasons for those in need. We adopted a local public school and a local private school within a stone's throw from our church and help resource and encourage them in their pursuits of loving and leading the next generation. We have meaningful relationships with local fire and police departments and with local businesses. Our people have embraced this at such a deep level that the community around us feels the shift. I could not be prouder to be a part of—let alone lead—a group of people than The MET Church.

That type of fruit is only born through alignment: when we all pull in a direction, stirred by a cause that is bigger than ourselves. This church has done it and continues to do it. It is a testimony to God's goodness and faithfulness to his promises. It is a testimony to the amazing people of this congregation. And it can be your testimony as well.

Epilogue

STAY THE COURSE

In Acts 27, we read about Paul's shipwreck on the way to Rome. As he and other prisoners traveled to Rome, they encountered a terrible storm. A wind of hurricane force drove the ship along its own course. The ship took a violent battering from the storm, and darkness enveloped the men for days. They were hungry, in the dark, and scared for their lives. Amid the trauma, Paul displayed leadership to these hungry, fearful men. He instilled hope in them once again by telling of how God's angel had promised him that no one would die. The ship eventually ran aground, but as God had promised Paul, no lives were lost, and everyone reached safety.

Although I have never been in an actual shipwreck, I can identify with so many aspects of this story as I retell the story of The MET and our journey toward relational discipleship. The deconstruction and rebuild was full of so many parallels with Acts 27. As it always does, God's Word speaks and sustains as we seek to fulfill the mission that he has given to us.

Face the Storms Head On

"We made slow headway for many days and had difficulty arriving off Cnidus. When the wind did not allow us to hold our course, we sailed to the isle of Crete, opposite Salmone. We moved along the coast with difficulty and came to a place called Fair Havens, near the town of Lasea" (Acts 27:7–8). Each storm you face may look different, but they all derail your progress in one way or another. You may have conflict among your leadership, loss of people within your congregation, or outside circumstances that attempt to keep you from achieving your mission. Moving toward your mission and creating a culture of meaningful relationship will require more time than you expect. So as you take ground, remember to celebrate. Celebrate each step you take—even if it's a small one—toward your mission. Build a culture of celebration within your leaders as well. It will propel you in the right direction even when you feel as though your progress has stagnated. Always keep the big picture in mind.

Paul always demonstrated a deep commitment to his mission. He had already had a long journey with Jesus, conceding that his life was not his own and his yes was on the table to whatever God had for him. His belief in the mission superseded his disappointment with the storms that kept him from making progress.

No doubt, at times the opposition, the length of time, and sheer magnitude of the shift were overwhelming and often tempted the leaders at The MET to give up. But experiencing the transformation and watching it in others will sustain the work and transition when circumstances get tough. Make sure you are staying close to the "God stories" and being refreshed by the evidence of the Spirit in people's lives, and not just putting out fires and fighting the battles day in and day out. This has been critical for me not to get discouraged.

Throw Off What Hinders

"So the soldiers cut the ropes that held the lifeboat and let it drift away" (Acts 27:32). In addition to storms, you may feel pressure from long-standing members of your congregation who rally to keep a particular ministry or program because of the positive impact it had on them. In previous seasons, I may have boldly and confidently cut off what I felt was holding us back, being confident of the bigger vision of where we were going. But now I realize *how* I lead people who don't see my vision is as critical as leading the change itself!

We, as leaders, must be practitioners of what we ask our people to practice. Relational discipleship isn't just fleshed out in our living rooms or back porches in small groups; it is who we are. It is who we are in elders' meetings, who we are with an angry church member, and who we are with a grieving Sunday school teacher. It manifests in how we treat people who slander us or leave our church without notice after we have invested in them relationally for years.

Some didn't receive the message Jesus preached, and he let them go their own way. So there's a tension that exists when leading change. Is this where I lean in and love through the painful conversation, accusations, and even hurtful engagement? Or is this where I simply allow someone to walk away? I will always feel this tension, and I will always need God's leadership in discerning between the two.

The Ship Will Not Look the Same

"But the ship struck a sandbar and ran aground. The bow stuck fast and would not move, and the stern was broken to pieces by the pounding of the surf. . . . The rest were to get there on planks or on other pieces of the ship. In this way everyone reached land safely" (Acts 27:41, 44). No doubt, your church will look different than it does today as you get into this process. Ministries may be pared down; members may leave; leaders and staff may get frustrated and upset; you may get weary and battle worn at times.

But be resolute in your commitment to carry out the mission that Jesus gave you. Your church will change. Your people will change. Your facilities will look different. Your Sunday services will feel different. But your goal must remain to make disciples of Jesus who go and do the same. Be willing to tear down whatever high places you must to remain obedient to God in your personal leadership and for his bride to experience all he has for her.

Don't Drift

I love the words to the old hymn "Come Thou Fount of Every Blessing":

Oh, to grace how great a debtor
Daily I'm constrained to be
Let Thy goodness like a fetter
Bind my wandering heart to Thee
Prone to wander, Lord, I feel it
Prone to leave the God I love
Here's my heart, oh take and seal it
Seal it for Thy courts above

My brother-in-law, John, and I were snorkeling in Hawaii. We waded out into the shallows, and before long we were swimming in water more than twenty feet deep. What we saw was simply stunning: all kinds of coral and some of the most colorful fish in the world, such as butterflyfish, yellow tangs, trumpetfish, angelfish, and many more. But I had one encounter that I will never forget. John tapped me on the shoulder as we snorkeled, and he pointed to my right. As I turned my head, a Hawaiian green sea turtle was within five feet of me, and not a small one either. The turtle almost appeared to yawn at me (which I found out later is a warning that I was swimming too close!), and I will never forget that feeling. In my panic, I sucked in some saltwater and had to surface for air.

But as I surfaced, I realized something: I was nowhere near where we had started. To our surprise, the sea had dragged us outward over half a mile. As we admired all that was under us, we failed to pay attention to where the current had taken us. We loved our time and in no way were in a dangerous situation, but the truth of that moment remains seared in my mind as a man, a husband, a father, and a leader. We are all prone to wander.

For so many leaders this is a defining reality. The need for approval, the draw toward success, insecurity, and so many other challenges often pull leaders away from truly following Jesus in their leadership. I am completely empathetic to the daily burdens and pulls on your heart and attention. I know you are a sinner and human. I know you don't want to be on a pedestal, and you get weary and sometimes want to phone it in. I hear you.

But I plead with you to stay anchored in Jesus' mission and methods. I validate God's calling on your life. He wants so much for his bride and the people he seeks to redeem. The waves of the sea drag leaders away from the mission to which Jesus orients them. If you aren't careful, you can spend most of your ministry staring at what many consider to be the fruit of ministry when you are actually wandering.

When my heart has set sail for a new destination other than Jesus Christ and his mission for the world, it drains so much energy, time, and resources. Following Jesus personally, as well as aligning our churches toward his mission, demands our all, doesn't it? Don't get swept away by the perceived fruit from programs of the past, the complaints of your people, or comparison with other churches. You'll look up one day and realize you are out to sea.

I pray blessings over you as you consider aligning both your life and your church to the principles in this book. My goal has been to share my story and The MET's story humbly and honestly as we set relational discipleship as the center of our focus. My prayer is that you and those you lead will experience the vibrancy, joy, and comfort of not doing life alone. Our world has never needed meaningful relationship with God and each other more than it does right now.

NOTES

1. *The Mandalorian*, 2019, season 1, episode 3, "Chapter 3: The Sin," directed by Deborah Chow, aired November 22, 2019, on Disney+.

2. *Merriam-Webster*, s.v. "meaningful (*adj.*)," accessed July 20, 2022, merriam-webster.com/dictionary/meaningful.

3. J. D. Greear, *Gaining by Losing: Why the Future Belongs to Churches That Send* (Grand Rapids: Zondervan, 2016), 20.

4. Samuel R. Chand, *Leadership Pain: The Classroom for Growth* (Nashville: Thomas Nelson, 2015), 5.

5. Daniel Im, *No Silver Bullets: 5 Small Shifts That Will Transform Your Ministry* (Nashville: B&H Publishing, 2017), 51–52.

6. Alexander Strauch, *Biblical Eldership: An Urgent Call to Restore Biblical Church Leadership* (Colorado Springs: Lewis and Roth Publishers, 2003), 111–112.

7. Brainy Quote, "Peter Drucker Quotes," accessed July 20, 2022, brainyquote.com/quotes/peter_drucker_134881.

8. Paul David Tripp, *Awe: Why It Matters for Everything We Think, Say, and Do* (Wheaton, IL: Crossway, 2015), 44.

9. Warren W. Wiersbe, *On Being a Leader for God* (Grand Rapids: Baker Books, 2011), 39.

ABOUT THE AUTHOR

MATT ROBERSON has served in multiple capacities in the local church—worship pastor, student pastor, and campus pastor in a multisite setting, and he is currently the senior pastor of The MET Church in Houston, Texas. He has the heart of a shepherd, is a gifted worship leader, a coach, and loves to lead change. Matt is married to Jennifer (June 2000), and they have two daughters, Chloe and Claire.

Made in the USA
Coppell, TX
27 November 2022

87175445R00079